Priceless

Priceless

Discovering True Love,

Beauty, and Confidence

By Chandra Peele

New Hope
PUBLISHERS
Birmingham, Alabama

New Hope® Publishers
P. O. Box 12065
Birmingham, AL 35202-2065
www.newhopepublishers.com

Library of Congress Cataloging-in-Publication Data
Peele, Chandra.
Priceless : discovering true love, beauty, and confidence / By Chandra Peele.
p. cm.
ISBN 1-56309-909-8 (pbk.)
1.   Teenage girls-Religious life. I. Title.
BV4551.3.P44 2005
248.8'33--dc22
2004024057

ISBN-10: 1-56309-909-8
ISBN-13: 978-1-56309-909-0

N054110 • 0409 • 1.5M6

About the Author:

With over 15 years in youth ministry, Chandra Peele has a high-energy style that attracts youth and keeps them interested. She addresses more than 8,000 students a year in churches, camps, conferences, and on local radio and TV in Texas. She is the founder of GAB (Godly and Beautiful) Ministries, which has sponsored numerous conferences for teen girls around the South. She is a certified abstinence trainer and has worked with Campus Life, Fellowship of Christian Athletes, Youth Specialties, True Love Waits, and See You at the Pole. She has monthly columns in the San Antonio Christian Beacon and in Planet Wisdom, an online magazine.

Peele served as a youth minister at Castle Hills Baptist Church in San Antonio from 1994–1999. She is the coauthor (with Aubrey Spears) of Great Love, a youth Bible study. She comes highly recommended by her pastor, Max Lucado; nationally-known youth speaker David Nasser; Stan Lee, founder of Dare 2 Run Ministries; and many other youth ministers who have invited Chandra to minister to their youth. Chandra and her husband, Bruce, live in Texas, and have two daughters.

www.gabministries.com

True Love! Who's interested in that? I bet you are. Girls simply want to know the facts about being "in love." So let's talk! There are so many misconceptions about what is right and what is wrong when it comes to sexual issues. I can remember when I was in fourth grade a fifth grade girl told me that if you French kiss you can get pregnant. Well, thankfully, I have learned a lot more about the birds and the bees since the fourth grade. I may be older than you and might not be as hip, but I can tell you one thing for sure—I know about true love. I am also sure that God's Word never changes and the dating tips you get in this book will be the truth. You can count on it. My greatest desires in ministry are:

- To encourage all girls to believe that they are beautiful and understand that they need Jesus to be their first love.
- To show girls how to be real and have fun being their adorable godly selves.
- To "gab" about dating and the importance of abstinence till marriage.

Learning more about these three topics can give you hope for a greater tomorrow and will allow you to live free in God's grace today!

Chandra

Table of Contents

Foreword

Teen years are a mountain path. Treacherous. Tight. Perilously close to the edge. You don't want to make this journey alone.

You don't have to. Chandra Peele will walk with you. The thick forests? She'll show you the meadow on the other side. The wide, white rivers? The bridge is just down the bank. A safe place to rest? Chandra knows where to find it.

She's helped thousands of young girls journey the trail, including my three daughters. My wife, Denalyn, and I have witnessed her passion firsthand. Chandra loves teens! She has the right word for this twisty time of life. God has guided her through the mountains and sent her back to do the same for others.

Do you fear the shadows? Feel confused at the many turns? Feel alone? Overwhelmed? If so, this is the book for you. Open up and step forth. The top of the mountain is closer than you think!

−Max Lucado

Love! True Love!

How exciting for me to be writing this introduction while preparing for Lindsey, my oldest daughter, to leave for college. One week from today our family will be loading up all our cars and moving her into an apartment. Of course there are many thoughts and memories rushing through my head, and emotions are at their highest level. Through it all there is one thing that keeps me going—Lindsey loves Jesus and He loves her. Knowing *that* is what helps me get through this "letting go" season of life.

What does this have to do with you or this Bible study? A whole lot! No matter who you are, what your family life is like, or how much you've messed up, Jesus loves you. Through reading the pages of this book you will begin to see that you really are *priceless*. Some of you will begin to understand your value for the first time, while others may just need a reminder.

Somehow when we get right down to it, we girls are so much alike. Not only do we have similarities in looks, dress, hair color, and style, we are also a lot alike on the inside. Deep down in our hearts we realize we are all the same. Needy for love. Needy for a Savior. Needy for Jesus.

Through the Father's wonderful love letters found in the Bible, together we will discover that we are not only His daughters but also the Bride of Christ. As we go through the journey of life, we are preparing for that day when we will trade in the materialistic fashion of today for fine white linen. Rags to riches? That's an understatement of what Jesus has for His bride. "Rejoice and be glad and give him glory! For the wedding of the Lamb has come, and his bride has made herself ready. Fine linen, bright and clean, was given her to wear" (Revelation 19:7–8). These words keep us hoping and longing with great expectations for the day the trumpet will sound. Joy!

In a world of twisted explanations of what *love* is, how comforting to know we can read the Bible (inspired by our Creator) and find the *real* meaning of *love*. As you journey through the pages of *Priceless*, you will see the light of His truth shining on you. If you open your heart, His tender hand of mercy and grace will give you a makeover inside out.

Through this process it may get a little uncomfortable as He begins to shine light on some dark areas. You will soon begin to notice how the choices you make today really do have a huge impact on your tomorrow. You can choose to do it your way, struggling as you mold and shape your future. Or you can decide to willingly turn your life over to Him, become like putty in His hands, allowing Him to do the molding. There is so much freedom when you trust Him. In the good times, the bad times, the "it's not fair" times, rejection, guilt and regret, aloneness, and wondering why you're here times; how wonderful to know that He will never leave you and never love you less than He already does. He keeps loving you, picking you up, dusting you off, cleaning you up, and carrying you when you just can't go on. And . . . it's His favorite thing to do!

Looking for love? God is love! Just as I have discovered that God can make the wrongs right, heal what is broken, and give direction in confusion, I am confident He wants to do the same for you.

The Map to Your Journey

Has someone ever asked you *"Are you born again?"* or *"Are you a Christian?"* and you really didn't know how to answer them? You may have visited a youth group or been to church with your friend and didn't say a word because you were confused or were afraid your answer would be wrong. Well, I'm sure most people can relate and have found themselves in the same situation. Not fun! You may have envisioned that you were on a game show and your answer is wrong. You turn red as a beet as bells and whistles go off and everyone is laughing at you. Or worse, someone bangs a huge gong! Well, walk with me through these pages and I'll try to give you the answers to all those tough questions.

How many times have you stood in line in a store for a free gift at the makeup counter? I have gotten so many of these that I now have a collection under my bathroom sink. These wonderful free gifts can quickly become worthless junk. And if you think about it, the cute little bags full of tiny samples are really not free at all. Think about how much you had to spend to get the "free gift!"

The free gift that Jesus offers is *really free*. You don't have to do anything or buy anything to receive it. All you need to do is believe it and eternal life is yours. You can accept this gift and begin a personal relationship with Jesus right now!

Before you continue this journey, it's important that you understand certain terminology that will be used as

The free gift that Jesus offers is really free.

you walk through these pages. When you go on a trip or vacation it's much easier when you have a road map. Being familiar with the words on the next few pages will help you to enjoy your trip through this book. Feel free to read this today and come back to fill in the answers as you proceed with your journey. However, make sure you read these pages entirely to ensure you have an opportunity to receive the free gift!

Sin—Sin is anything you do, think, or say that is against God's teaching. You and me—each one of us—have sinned. We all have to admit that we are sinners. There are no perfect people. Jesus is the only one who lived on this Earth who was perfect.

"For all have sinned and fall short of the glory of God."
—Romans 3:23

Grace—Grace is a gift. The greatest gift of all is eternal life through Jesus. He died on the cross so that you might live forever!

"For it is by grace you have been saved, through faith—and this not from yourselves, it is the gift of God—not by works, so that no one can boast."
—Ephesians 2:8–9

Jesus—Jesus is the perfect Son of God, who died on the cross for you and me. God could have saved Him, but there had to be a perfect sacrifice to pay the penalty for our sin. Jesus chose to die for you. He knew it was the only way you could live with Him forever in heaven.

The greatest gift of all is eternal life through Jesus.

That's how much He loves you!

"For God so loved the world that he gave his one and only Son, that whoever believes in him shall not perish but have eternal life."
—John 3:16

Faith—Faith is believing in things unseen. Grace is a gift from God and so is the faith it takes to believe. Graciously accept this gift and be thankful to God, the one who gives the gift. Look at your pinky finger. It is little and weak, just like you without faith. But with faith, you are mighty and strong because of the power of God through Jesus. Supernatural power!

"For it is by grace you have been saved, through faith—and this not from yourselves, it is the gift of God—not by works, so that no one can boast."
—Ephesians 2:8–9

Holy Spirit—When Jesus left this earth to be with God the Father in heaven, He sent the Holy Spirit to dwell in those who would accept Him as the Messiah, the Son of the one and only true God. Those who by faith believe are empowered with the Holy Spirit as a counselor and guide.

I once heard someone give this example and I think it goes great with teaching you about the Holy Spirit. Imagine a pair of work gloves. These gloves don't just go out to the garden and plant, dig, or pull weeds by themselves. Of course not! They are useless until you put your hands in them. Your hands give power to the gloves so they can do the work. It's the same way with the Holy Spirit. You and I can walk and talk and live without the Holy Spirit; however, without Jesus, many times we feel empty and useless. With the Holy Spirit in us, we've got the power! Now we are empowered by the Holy Spirit, which is Christ in us.

Righteous—Righteous means good, pure, holy, and perfect. The only way a person is righteous is through the blood that was shed for you and me on the cross by our Savior, Jesus.

"This righteousness from God comes through faith in Jesus Christ to all who believe."
Romans 3:22

Repent—Repent is an action word. You recognize your sin and turn away (I mean a complete 180 degrees). You leave your old ways completely behind.

"Repent, then, and turn to God, so that your sins may be wiped out, that times of refreshing may come from the Lord."
—Acts 3:19

Forgiveness—God is merciful. He forgives us from all our sin when we turn over our lives to Him. He doesn't hold grudges or remember our wrongs. Forgiveness! Wow! What a great thing to experience.

"If we confess our sins, he is faithful and just and will forgive us our sins and purify us from all unrighteousness."
—1 John 1:9

With the Holy Spirit in us, we've got the power!

Restoration—Restoration is one of His specialties. Restoration means to make new again.

Eternal Life—To live forever in a place called heaven!

"No eye has seen, no ear has heard, no mind has conceived what God has prepared for those who love him."
—1 Corinthians 2:9

Salvation—Trusting Jesus as your Savior and being delivered from the power and penalty of sin. Salvation is available for any who put their trust in Christ as Savior. (See Romans 3:23–24, Romans 6:23.) **Redemption** is another word that means the same thing.

"That if you confess with your mouth, 'Jesus is Lord,' and believe in your heart that God raised him from the dead, you will be saved."
—Romans 10:9

GAB Session
~ with Chandra ~

Every night about ten o'clock I let my dog Reeses out. She usually comes back to the door right away, but on one particular night, she didn't. I opened the door and called for her but she didn't come. I began to worry when I spotted her sitting very still with her eyes closed. I ran to her, picked her up, and realized she had been sprayed by a skunk right in the face and couldn't see! This was why she couldn't respond to my call. By this time, I put her down, choking on the smell, whereupon she proceeded to run into the house, rubbing her nose and body all over the carpet. Everyone in the house was calling out, "What's that smell?" Immediately, I remembered my granddaddy telling me that tomato juice would get rid of a skunk's smell.

I trekked to the store late at night only to find it was closed! Since they had just locked their doors, I pleaded with the manager to please get me a couple of cans of tomato juice. He believed my story because a strong skunk smell was seeping its way through the door. Thankfully he got me my juice and I was on my way to bathe Reeses. As I started the water and opened the can of tomato juice, I thought, "Lord, maybe I can get a message out of this tonight, a funny story to share." I was amazed how quickly He answered that prayer. As I poured the tomato juice onto Reeses, it gave me chills to see the water in the tub turn blood red.

God spoke to my heart very clearly at that moment. The only thing that can take skunk smell out of a dog is tomato juice. Nothing else will do it. The only thing that can wash away my sin is the blood of Jesus. Nothing else will do it. That night I saw how His cleansing was immediate and complete. What an awesome picture of what He did for me.

The skunk smell could not be hidden. It was pretty

The only thing that can wash away my sin is the blood of Jesus.

obvious to everyone around. What about sin? Some sin is obvious. Some sin is well hidden. But nothing is hidden from God.

Take a moment here and write down your sin on a piece of paper. This is just between you and God. Think about it and write even the little sin. (Isn't it funny how we categorize sin?) After you have written it down, read it to yourself. Now take the paper and destroy it. Read this Scripture as you do so and be reminded of God's love for you.

"For as high as the heavens are above the earth, so great is his love for those who fear him; as far as the east is from the west, so far has he removed our transgressions from us."
—Psalm 103:11–12

Has there ever been a time when you asked Jesus to take over your life? A time when you let Him have the driver's seat of your life? Have you ever told Him, "Jesus, I believe that You are the Son of God and I accept Your grace as a free gift, knowing I can't earn it." If you have never expressed this but would like to, you can accept His invitation today. This is the "free gift" He offers. Share your decision with someone that you know has a growing relationship with Jesus. They will celebrate with you and welcome you into the family of God!

The next step is to be baptized. This is a symbolic action to show that you are a new creation in Christ. Now the spirit of Jesus lives in you. You will be changed, renewed, forgiven, and *free*! You can now live a life of hope. Jesus is the driver of your life, your captain, your pilot.

Jesus is the driver of your life, your captain, your pilot.

What is the most memorized verse of the Bible other than the 23rd Psalm? Look at John 3:16. Make it personal by putting your name in place of *"the world."*

There is assurance in salvation through Jesus. This is our hope!

Chandra

The Most Beautiful Love Story of All

"I delight greatly in the Lord; my soul rejoices in my God. For he has clothed me with garments of salvation and arrayed me in a robe of righteousness, as a bridegroom adorns his head like a priest, and as a bride adorns herself with her jewels."

–Isaiah 61:10

There will come a day when most of you *godly and beautiful* young ladies will be proposed to. You will be chosen. Can you imagine that? Most young girls dream about their wedding day long before they ever have a boyfriend. How wonderful to be chosen, to be spoken for. I'm talking about the kind of love that is always and forever, when that special man takes you by the hand, looks into your eyes, and asks, "Will you marry me?" But wait a minute. Does the proposal automatically make you his bride-to-be? No. You have to accept the invitation and say, "Yes, I will marry you."

This same story can be identified with your relationship to God right now. The Creator of the world, the

There is a King—not just any King—the King of all Kings, and He has a Son.

His son, the Prince, is a perfect Son, and the King desires for Him to have a bride.

God of the universe, the King of the world chooses you. He wants to call you His own. He wants to be your first love, your everything. Do you know that the Bible calls the church the *Bride of Christ*? Just like you have to answer the marriage proposal, you have to accept God's proposal. God will wait until you are ready. One thing for sure is that the Bridegroom (Jesus) is coming, and the wedding reception is being set into place and has been since the beginning of time. We need to be preparing for the biggest day of our lives. We never know when the trumpets will sound and the Bridegroom will come to claim His bride.

Look at Revelation 19:7-8. Who do you think is referred to as the bride who has prepared herself?

_____

_____

_____

_____

_____

Are you a part of the church? Are you a child of God? Then you are the Bride of Christ. Isn't that a wonderful name to have? God desires for you, as the Bride of Christ, to give yourself to His Son, Jesus, above anyone else. He wants Jesus to be your first love.

God the Father says, "I promise to give you to Christ, as your only husband. I want to give you as a pure bride. His bride must be very special. She needs to be pure and untouched. She must wear the *proper wedding clothes.*"

So what are the proper wedding clothes? Well, first let me tell you what they are not. They are not found on the cover of a popular bride magazine, and they can't be purchased in the finest bridal boutique in your town. They aren't material objects at all. You can't buy them with all the money in the world.

So what are they and where can you get them?

You can only receive these clothes as a *gift* from **Jesus**. You see, God knew He would never find the perfect bride for His Son because of sin in the world. The only way it could happen was through His only Son, Jesus.

In clothes of righteousness— this is how we can be properly dressed for the wedding.

Remember, we aren't talking about shopping in this session. These clothes are given to us as a free gift. Jesus paid a very high price when He gave His life to pay for our sin. When you accept this invitation, Jesus gives you new clothes. He exchanges your old filthy rags with His coat of righteousness. As your relationship with Him grows, you will become more like Him. It becomes your desire to have:

• Godly morals
• Higher standards

If we are "in Him," then we should reflect that inside-out. God wants our heart, our complete love and devotion.

It says in Isaiah 64:6, "all our righteous acts are like filthy rags." Do you understand what your righteous acts are? A few examples are: going to church, helping out a neighbor, or giving all our money to the poor. These are all great things to do! But by themselves, they do not make us righteous; they are only righteous deeds.

Do you have some deeds you claim as righteous? This is a hard question, because I think we do a lot of **works** for the praise of people rather than doing them with a pure heart because of our passion for Christ.

1. Go to youth group

2. Obey my parents

3. Memorize Bible verses

4. _____

5. _____

6. _____

7. _____

8. _____

9. _____

10. _____

Take some time to rethink why you do these things. Is it for the praise of those around you or to pat yourself on

We can't earn righteousness, and we don't deserve it!

the back for being so righteous, or is it to glorify God? Isn't it an awesome thought that no matter how good or how rotten our deeds, none of what we **do** is going to get us brownie points with God?

You may ask: If we don't have to work for these clothes, then why does it seem like there are certain things we have to do? Good question! People that don't know Jesus can't understand it. That is why faith is the key to an intimate relationship with Him. When we become filled with the Spirit (the Holy Spirit lives in us), we are a new creation. These are things we gladly do because we want to please our Father.

As a princess, a daughter of the King, we want to be obedient and please Him. Think of your earthly father. My daddy was very special to me. Pleasing him was something I put high on my 'to do list.' When Daddy wasn't happy with me, believe me, I knew it. The tears in my eyes when I got in trouble for disobedience were not my attempt of pity. They were there because I knew I let him down.

Is there a time that comes to your mind when you let your earthly father down? What happened and how did it make you feel?

_____

_____

_____

_____

_____

"He himself bore our sins in his body on the tree, so that we might die to sins and live for right- eousness; by his wounds you have been healed."
— *1 Peter 2:24*

*Jesus is the **King of the World**! And the King of the World chooses you! Isn't that awesome?*

We want to be like Jesus so that God the Father will be pleased with us. God knows us so well that He knew we couldn't be obedient all the time, but the bride for His Son had to be perfect. This is why He sacrificed Jesus, His only Son. He knew we needed His grace and mercy to be clothed in righteousness.

You see, we must be clothed in His righteousness to enter the kingdom of heaven. We can only do that through the blood of Jesus. He was the one and only perfect sacrifice.

1 Peter 2:24 tells us that Jesus died for you and me on the cross. He took the sins of each of us on Himself—the sins of the whole world. He Himself bore our sin in His body on the tree that we might die to sin and live for righteousness.

What did Jesus do for you and me to provide the perfect wedding clothes?

_____

_____

_____

_____

_____

_____

_____

Jeremiah 31:3–4 says that He (God) loves you with an everlasting love.

> "The LORD appeared to us in the past, saying: 'I have loved you with an everlasting love; I have drawn you with loving-kindness. I will build you up again and you will be rebuilt, O Virgin Israel. Again you will take up your tambourines and go out to dance with the joyful.'"
>
> —Jeremiah 31:3–4

Who is He talking about when He says, "O Virgin Israel"?

_____

_____

_____

_____

_____

Who does He love with an everlasting love?

_____

_____

_____

_____

_____

Compare this passage in Jeremiah with Isaiah 4:2-6. Write down your findings.

_____

_____

_____

_____

_____

_____

God wants to restore His people. He loves us and restores us unto Himself.

"In that day the Branch of the LORD will be beautiful and glorious, and the fruit of the land will be the pride and glory of the survivors in Israel. Those who are left in Zion, who remain in Jerusalem, will be called holy, all who are recorded among the living in Jerusalem. The Lord will wash away the filth of the women of Zion; he will cleanse the bloodstains from Jerusalem by a spirit of judgment and a spirit of fire. Then the LORD will create over all of Mount Zion and over those who assemble there a cloud of smoke by day and glow of flaming fire by night; over all the glory will be a canopy. It will be a shelter and shade from the heat of the day, and a refuge and hiding place from the storm and rain."
—Isaiah 4:2–6

FYI-The Church is also called the Remnant. This means that the people of God are not identified with a nation but are obedient, faithful worshipers of God. They may, however, still hang out with those who are not faithful.

Okay, let me explain. You go to youth group, school, and other places where there are a lot of people you know. Some of these people claim to be Christians; however, they don't walk it, talk it, or live it out. You see them one way at church and another at a party. This makes you wonder if they really know the Lord. It may be that they do not fully understand their salvation or they may never have grown in their faith. Others may have never even given their hearts to God. In other words, sometimes we don't know whether or not another person knows God. Therefore we must be a witness to them.

We are the people of God!

We are the Bride of Christ! It should be our desire to present ourselves holy and pure before the Father. We can only do that through Jesus Christ, through His righteousness, which is spiritual purity.
The blood of Jesus washed us white as snow.
- No more sin.
- No more shame/guilt.
- No more bondage to guilt from our past.

❤

The Bridegroom is coming back for you and for me.

Trading Rags for Riches

I lost my daddy to cancer. It was very hard for my family as we watched him suffer and fight the disease for fifteen months. My daddy wasn't ready to leave us but in the end he was ready to meet Jesus. I have a robe that is very precious to me. My daddy wore this robe throughout his illness to cover his frail body. Isn't it funny how something so worthless is so priceless to me now? But do you know that in the end it didn't matter what my daddy was wearing? It didn't matter that it was an inexpensive robe. It wouldn't have even mattered if it was worth a thousand dollars. The only thing that mattered is that many years ago, he had exchanged his filthy rags for a coat of righteousness. That coat was given to him by Jesus when my daddy accepted Him as Savior and made Jesus Lord of his life. My daddy traded sin for grace in the form of a white robe—a covering of righteousness. This robe can't be purchased at any store. It can't be bought at any price. It has already been paid for with a very high price, the blood of Jesus. As great as I thought my daddy was, he wasn't good enough to earn his way into heaven. He had to receive the gift of grace, and Jesus gives it freely to all those who accept it.

All that mattered to my daddy in the end was a desire to go home. He was ready to see Jesus. Now his address is Golden Street, Heaven. I'm so glad my daddy was dressed in the proper clothes for the wedding celebration that was given to him as he entered the gates of heaven. Now I have the promise that I will see him again.

What about you? Have you traded your clothes in? Are you dressed for the wedding? Are you dressed in

I have a robe that is very precious to me.

His righteousness?

The *Bride of Christ* is all men, women, boys, and girls who have accepted this invitation. There will be a day when Jesus comes to take His bride to the greatest wedding celebration ever. I pray that your heart is open wide. I pray that you understand this message of hope.

When you accept this invitation, God sees you as the Bride of Christ. This isn't a promise for the wealthy and educated but to all those who are clothed in Christ.

Be clothed

in Christ!

GAB Session
~ with Chandra ~

Have you ever been to a garage sale? They are really fun, especially when you find a treasure. One particular day I was in search of a dresser for my daughter Lindsey. We looked at several garage sales and had no luck. My husband, Bruce, had all he could take and was ready to head back home. Shopping was the last thing he had on his "to do" list for Saturday. I was disappointed but knew there would be another day for hunting and perhaps a better day for dresser shopping.

On that Sunday at church, I overheard a friend sharing that she had been busy getting things ready for an estate sale and would be selling furniture. Well, that was just what I needed to hear. I asked her if I could go over early and she agreed. Walking into her garage I saw what I had been looking for—an antique dresser. The wood was dry and scratched here and there, and it had a couple of drink rings on the top, but for $75 it would do. For two years the dresser worked great for Lindsey, but then we moved. In the new house there was a perfect place for the dresser, but it would be in a place where we saw it often. I decided to have it restored. To my surprise, it was beautiful! The mahogany was restored to perfection. The wood grain and every detail of the dresser seemed perfectly new and could be

Dear Jesus,

Thank You for loving me unconditionally. Thank You for the Holy Spirit, who gives me power and strength. Lead me and direct me to be an overcomer of the things of this world. I worship You and You alone, for You are great and mighty and worthy of all my praise. God, help me to be content with You alone. Teach me to live by faith and walk by faith so I will follow You all the days of my life. Help me to hunger and thirst for Your righteousness so I may be blessed by You (Matthew 5:6). In Jesus' name I pray. Amen enjoyed by all who visited our home. The carpenter said that it was one of the most beautiful pieces he had ever restored.

Isn't it amazing how some old dresser left out in a garage, considered junk to someone, could now become of great worth once it was restored? That is just like you and me. We can feel worthless, lonely, and good for nothing on our own. But amazingly, when God restores us, we are of great worth to Him.

Our greatest treasure is not found in material things, but in a relationship with Jesus.

Matthew 6:21 says, "For where your treasure is, there your heart will be also."

It's not a fairy tale. It's true! Jesus loves you! The reason this is the greatest love story of all is because it's about God's love for **you**. Imagine you are all alone, feeling _____ (insert the word that fits your life). You drop to your knees and begin to call out to Jesus. You sit silently, unsure of what to say. With tears running down your face, you suddenly feel two warm hands under your chin; they gently tilt your head upward. It's Jesus. As He looks at you, He tenderly says, "Daughter, I am enthralled by your beauty. I love you. You are mine for all eternity and I am with you always."

You are priceless!
Me too!

Chandra

My Journal

My Journal

My Journal

~~~~~~

~~~~~~

~~~~~~

~~~~~~

~~~~~~

~~~~~~

~~~~~~

~~~~~~

~~~~~~

~~~~~~

~~~~~~

~~~~~~

My Journal

White As Snow

"Your beauty should not come from outward adornment, such as braided hair and the wearing of gold jewelry and fine clothes. Instead, it should be that of your inner self, the unfading beauty of a gentle and quiet spirit, which is of great worth in God's sight." –1 Peter 3:3-4

What does purity mean to you?

Think about the most beautiful snow-capped mountain you have ever seen. Some of you have seen one in person—maybe you've actually climbed up to the top. Others of you have only seen beautiful mountains in pictures. Have you ever noticed that they are bald on top? Most of the year there is snow on them and the ground is so cold that nothing can grow on the peaks. The snow glistens and sparkles out of reach to people and most animals. As you envision that snow-white covered mountain peak, think *purity*. Why? What a great picture to have in our minds of something untouched; something pure.

In Webster's Dictionary the definition of *purity* is: "The quality of being pure; freedom from guilt or sin."

The definition of *pure* is: "Free from anything that damages, weakens, or contaminates; innocent; clean."

That is exactly what we are going to discuss today.

We don't hear this word used much today because, well, think about it…

What do you know that is pure?

_____

_____

_____

_____

_____

_____

❤

"But just as he who called you is holy, so be holy in all you do."

—_1 Peter 1:15_

In our first session, we talked about spiritual purity—**righteousness**. In this session, we are going to apply the principle of **purity** to your physical body. It is pretty tough to stay physically pure today. Keeping your mouth, mind, and body pure is a moment-by-moment challenge. Just like cleanliness is important for your body, it is also very important for your mind. I think you would agree that the grace of Jesus is pretty awesome when we consider He loves us through all our impure thoughts and judgments of others.

Think about your body for a minute. It can get pretty dirty and smelly, right? Now think about your mind. Maybe this is a wake-up call for you. Your mind can get pretty dirty and smelly too. Ugly thoughts, selfish desires, jealousy, etc . . .

I want you to only think about yourself right now (remember: this journey is for you). Looking at God's Word on these difficult topics will help you look at the real you, and the Holy Spirit will probably _tweak_ (my word for bursting your bubble) you some.

What must you personally do to have purity?

To be holy as God is holy is an impossible task without Jesus. Peter is such a great teacher and he helps us to understand in 2 Peter 1:3–8 how to lead a godly life.

"His divine power has given us everything we need for life and godliness through our knowledge of him who called us by his own glory and goodness. Through these he has given us his very great and precious promises, so that through them you may participate in the divine nature and escape the corruption in the world caused by evil desires.

"For this very reason, make every effort to add to your faith goodness…knowledge…self-control…perseverance… godliness…brotherly kindness…love.

"For if you possess these qualities in increasing measure, they will keep you from being ineffective and unproductive in your knowledge of our Lord Jesus Christ."

We must remember that *purity is a process*. We are a work in progress, and chances are, we will be challenged daily in the area of purity.

My relationship with the Lord is precious and the most important thing to me. There have been times when I allowed my heart to become hard, and sin has kept me from an intimate relationship with Jesus. This sin built up and kept me from talking with the Lord like I had before. Our relationship felt distant because of the sin in my life. But God's love was so great that He pursued me until He got my attention. You may be able to relate to this story . . .

♥

We are a work in progress, and chances are, we will be challenged daily in the area of purity.

Patty's Parent Problems

Patty was usually a good girl who never got into much trouble, until one day when she decided to skip last period and go to the mall with her friends. She knew this was a direct act of disobedience to her parents and their rules. Afterwards, Patty felt terrible about what she had done. She spent days sneaking around trying to avoid those eye-to-eye discussions with her parents, because she couldn't bear to face them. One night she came in late. She tried to sneak into the house through the back door, hoping her parents wouldn't hear her, and suddenly the dark room lit up, and there they were. Patty was caught. The sneaking was over, and they confronted her with everything.

She became very angry and defensive. "How dare they get on to me," she thought. Her punishment was that she couldn't go out for a month on the weekends, and she was not a happy camper.

After having a bad attitude and ignoring her parents for a few days, she admitted it was her actions that got her into trouble and that she deserved the punishment given. Later that week, Patty admitted to her parents that she had been disobedient. She apologized to her parents, took the punishment, and realized how great it was to confess the truth. She was so tired of sneaking around and covering up one lie after another. After confessing, she realized what a weight had been lifted off her shoulders. She realized she hadn't been herself in weeks. The freedom she was experiencing was great! She was reminded that her parents really do have her best interests in mind when giving rules and setting boundaries, because they love her.

❤

"But the wisdom that comes from heaven is first of all pure; then peace-loving, considerate, submissive, full of mercy and good fruit, impartial and sincere. Peacemakers who sow in peace raise a harvest of righteousness."

—James 3:17–18

Sound familiar? I think we've all been in this place. Disobedience to our heavenly Father is very much the same. We think we can handle things on our own, and before we know it, we begin to rationalize the situation (the sin) to make us feel better until one day we realize our relationship with Jesus is not good—we have no joy and no peace. When things are caving in all around us, then we cry out to God.

Sin keeps you away from the Lord and keeps you from being effective for Him. It also keeps you from having a pure heart.

Are you rubbing off on others or are they rubbing off on you?

At the very end of 2 Corinthians 6, Paul is warning the Corinthian believers to be careful when hanging out with non-believers. He encourages us to be active in our witness to non-believers but not to have binding relationships with them.

Common sense is pretty obvious here. When we are hanging out with a majority of people who don't know Jesus, they obviously don't have the same goals we have. No doubt it will hinder our relationship and witness for the Lord. Look with me starting at 2 Corinthians 6:16 through the end of chapter 6.

"What agreement is there between the temple of God and idols? For we are the temple of the living God. As God has said: 'I will live with them and walk among them, and I will be their God, and they will be my people.' 'Therefore come out from them and be separate....Touch no unclean thing, and I

will receive you.' 'I will be a Father to you, and you will be my sons and daughters, says the Lord Almighty.'"

Now keep reading through the first verse of chapter 7.

"Since we have these promises, dear friends, let us purify ourselves from everything that contaminates body and spirit, perfecting holiness out of reverence for God."

If you and I desire to be pleasing to our God, here it is plain and simple. Some people tell me they just can't understand the Bible. To me this is pretty clear and certainly applies to our lives today. Paul is encouraging us to live godly lives according to what **Jesus** said.

• Perfecting holiness.

• Turning away from sin and toward God.

   Below are some areas of purity where I think we can all use some guidance.

The Tongue

Let's begin with how you talk.

"But no man can tame the tongue. It is a restless evil, full of deadly poison."
—James 3:8.

Why would James say this about the tongue?

_____

_____

_____

_____

_____

_____

_____

_____

Is it a true statement in your life and how does it apply to your relationships?

Parents

_____

_____

_____

_____

_____

_____

Siblings

_____

_____

_____

_____

_____

_____

_____

❤

"I said, 'I will watch my ways, and keep my tongue from sin; I will put a muzzle on my mouth as long as the wicked are in my presence.'"

—Psalm 39:1

Friends

_____

_____

_____

_____

_____

Acquaintances

_____

_____

_____

_____

_____

Read Psalm 39:1 and write your thoughts concerning the muzzle.

_____

_____

_____

_____

_____

I think we all agree that it is hard to be human—a girl—and have a pure tongue. Like I said, this purity thing is a daily process!

The Mind

Apply this to your thoughts.

How many times just today have you had impure thoughts?
(Example: ugly thoughts about a stranger, jealousy of a friend, attitude towards your parents or teacher, ignoring a person in need, etc.)

_____

What do you need to do when these thoughts come to your mind?

_____

_____

_____

_____

_____

_____

God is not glorified by these thoughts. Imagine Satan sitting back eating bon-bons as he watches you create a soap opera of your own life.

Look up Psalm 40 and read it now. You could sing these same words today. Okay, don't let this be like a homework assignment. However, I'd like you to take some time and write down how this chapter applies to your life. It may be just a couple verses. You could write a poem, a song, whatever you like. Remember, your current circumstances may be very different from what others are going through. As you write, write to God.

*You can share your writing with others or keep it to

yourself. May God bless you as you study and apply His Word to your life.

_____

_____

_____

_____

_____

_____

The Body

I thought about writing a book just about purity of the body. There are so many issues to deal with when talking about our bodies. Keeping the body pure is very difficult and very easily forgotten because of our worldly surroundings (i.e. movies, magazines, prime time TV, internet, music, chat room discussions, movie stars, trends, etc.)

In this session, we are not dealing with sexual purity. Although that is a huge part of physical purity, there are so many other areas we seem to overlook. Many girls become obsessed with their bodies. Instead of giving it over to God, they allow the world's outlook and latest trend to become what they reflect through the choices they make about their bodies.

Looking at magazines is not a bad thing. However, becoming addicted to the things you see in the magazine is the problem I want to warn you against. This is another area we are tempted to worship something other than God (that means we put something above Him.)

We are tempted to worship things other than God.

List some things that could cause you to struggle with keeping your body pure.

_____

_____

_____

_____

_____

_____

I recently saw a magazine headline, "Cute or Sexy—To Be or Not to Be?" This was a real eye opener for me. The whole world is selling out to sexy, but I like cute!

List words you can think of that go along with:

Sexy   **Cute**

_____   _____

_____   _____

_____   _____

_____   _____

_____   _____

_____   _____

The list was pretty easy to fill in, right? Now let me ask you this: Why would you want to be sexy more than cute? Look at the list of words you created, and see which words reflect a _godly and beautiful_ young lady and which words don't. I think it is pretty obvious which list God would like to see His daughters be. Remember, girls, you are the daughter of the King. Can you imagine a sleazy princess? Yuk! I think she would lose her crown.

One Bad Choice

Some of you may have heard the story of Vanessa Williams. She was crowned Miss America, but because of a bad choice she made earlier in her life, her crown and title were taken away. Vanessa had chosen to pose nude in a popular men's magazine, and to the Board of Miss America, it was cause for immediate dismissal. Miss America is to be known for setting an example of good character and has a high standard of values that can be respected by all Americans. The title "Miss America" represents the people of America to others all over the world.

The consequences of immorality always come back around.

Why do you think some girls desire to be sexy?

_____

_____

_____

_____

_____

_____

_____

_____

Remember,

you are the daughter

of the King!

When do you have these desires, if ever? (It is true that some girls struggle here more than others.)

_____

_____

_____

_____

_____

_____

How does it make you feel when there is a girl around you who looks sexy?

_____

_____

_____

_____

_____

_____

Around your guy friends?

_____

_____

_____

_____

_____

_____

Around your boyfriend?

_____

_____

_____

_____

_____

Does being "sexy" fit anywhere in the verse below? I don't think so.

"Finally, brothers, whatever is true, whatever is noble, whatever is right, whatever is pure, whatever is lovely, whatever is admirable—if anything is excellent or praiseworthy—think about such things....put it into practice."
—Philippians 4:8–9

Ladies, let me encourage you to read God's Word and hide it in your heart so that you might not sin against Him. In the way you dress, if you can't check off all the words mentioned in the verse above when you look in the mirror, simply don't wear it! If you put this into practice now, God will bless you. And when you are shopping, you will begin to notice that you will stop being drawn to outfits that aren't appropriate for the *godly and beautiful* you.

God's Word tells us that we live in the world, but we shouldn't conform to the world. We need to have high standards so we will shine in the darkness. If you begin today choosing these high godly standards (that show

♥

We need to have high standards so we will shine in the darkness.

Christ-like character), I know God will bless you. Chances are really good that you will be happier too.

Remember our key verse for this study:

"Your beauty should not come from outward adornment, such as braided hair and the wearing of gold jewelry and fine clothes. Instead, it should be that of your inner self, the unfading beauty of a gentle and quiet spirit, which is of great worth in God's sight." –1 Peter 3:3-4

GAB Session
~ with Chandra ~

Father, today I ask You to purify the hearts of all those who read this. May Your words bring Your daughter peace and hope this day, and may she see Your love for her. Give her the desire to have a pure heart and clean hands and to look for Your truth in everything that comes her way. Oh God, may she receive the blessing You promise and see purity in her life today.

Amen

As your big sis in Christ, I'd like to share with you what I have learned about purity. First of all, there is no way you or I can be pure. Jesus is the only perfect, pure one who has walked upon this earth. So, why do we say we want to be pure? Because, through Jesus, we can strive to be pure. Being holy is not being perfect. Instead it is realizing that He who lives in you is holy and because of that, we can be holy. Sin has no power over us if we belong to Jesus. However, we can let our sin nature lead us to bad choices. For holiness and purity to be manifest in our lives, we must believe that "those who belong to Christ Jesus have crucified the sinful nature with its passions and desires" (Galatians 5:24). Holiness means to be separated from the ways of the world. Being purified is a process, as we've discussed in this session. Run to the things of God, and allow Him to purify your thoughts and your actions. If we simply put on a white robe, we are covering up a lot of impurities. This sounds really gross, but it's kind of like cleaning the pores of your face. To have clean pores and a nice complexion that is smooth and silky, you have to open up your pores and get the blackheads out. Yuck! I know. But it's so true. Just like a blackhead, you can cover sin up again and again, but at some point it turns really ugly, and you can no longer hide it. Then after you get it out of your skin, whew! You're rid of it. This is like the sin in our lives. At some point, sin is always revealed. That's why—as your big sis—I encourage you to be open with Jesus. Allow Him to purify your heart each day so you will know what is pure and what is impure.

Throughout my life, I have realized that reading His Word, talking with Him, and confessing my impure thoughts and actions keep me closer to Him and more on track with His will for my life.

"Create in me a pure heart, O God, and renew a steadfast spirit within me."
—Psalm 51:10

Longing for holiness,

Chandra

My Journal

My Journal

My Journal

My Journal

My Journal

session 3

Why Is Having a Boyfriend So Important?

"Love is patient . . ."
–1 Corinthians 13:4

One summer, when my daughter Lindsey was 16, she had several friends over (four boys and three girls). When it got late, she asked if they could stay later to watch a movie and just hang out (I'm talking really late!). My husband Bruce and I discussed it, and we agreed. Lindsey and her friends were so excited! I want you to understand that I would not have allowed just any boys this privilege. These kids have earned the respect of my husband and myself, and we have watched them grow into responsible young men. Besides, there were no couples involved; they where all just really good friends.

With 16- and 17-year-old girls and guys hanging out, you can imagine the flirting going on. As a mom feeling responsible, do you think I got any sleep that night? Of course not! There was loud laughing, stomping on the floor along with other weird noises, the movie was loud, and every once in a while I would even hear laughing interrupted with screaming. What were they doing?

It's hard being a parent. You really need to respect and appreciate your parents. I have to remind my girls all the time that I will trust them as long as they continue to be obedient. But I was once a teenager, and I am well aware of the thoughts that go through the young teenage mind.

"So what did you guys do last night, Lindsey?" I asked casually the next morning while fixing cheese omelets and toast for the girls.

Lindsey gushed, "Mom, we had so much fun! Thank you for letting them stay so late. We tickled and wrestled with the guys. [Hum . . . didn't exactly know how I felt about that.] They ate, and then strange noises started coming out of their bodies and we laughed and laughed. Then we watched a movie and just hung out."

In a quieter voice, she added, "I wish I had a boyfriend, Mom. It would be so fun to have a guy to hang out with all the time."

It is fun hanging out with guys. I admit it; I loved it when I was a teenager, too. Many of my close friends were guys. My girls have heard me say many times, "Having guys for friends instead of boyfriends is the way to go. It will save you from a lot of tears." What I mean by that is pretty obvious. If you are just friends, like Lindsey and those boys, you can be yourself. You

It is fun hanging out with guys. I admit it.

can hang out and act crazy then say, "I'll see you tomorrow." When you are going out and you say, "See you tomorrow," you may wonder if he will change his mind about going out with you by then. You also begin to make little things into big things. "Why didn't he call last night?" "He's not talking to me enough!" Man, these little things can send you on a long emotional trip. That kind of relationship isn't good and it's sure not worth it.

Why Be in a Hurry?

I was in youth ministry for several years at a church in San Antonio, Texas. I developed some great relationships with students during my time there. I have been able to keep in touch with a few of them over the years. Some are just getting married and others are starting families of their own. What a blessing to see them grow up into mature adults as they continue to grow in the Lord.

While getting together with a few of the girls recently, one of them shared her desire to give her perspective on dating during high school.

"Being concerned with boyfriends takes away from the time and energy you could be putting into your youth group and extra-curricular activities," she noted. "If I had dated seriously through high school, I would have missed out on so many awesome, worry-free weekends and trips!"

During her college years, she dated several guys, but I am happy to tell you that during her senior year of college she fell in love with a godly young man and they were soon married. What an honor it was when the bride asked Bruce and me to be a part of the wedding ceremony. Much to my surprise I had the opportunity to witness something unexpected before the ceremony. Just before the wedding a gift arrived from the groom for his bride. Wrapped in a beautiful white gift bag was his "True Love Waits" commitment card that he had signed six years earlier. He had honored his commitment, was obedient to God's plan, and was confident that God would bless his marriage. Everyone in the room had tears of joy as we realized what a priceless gift he had given her.

My friend was right! There is plenty of time for you to meet Mr. Right. There is no need to be anxious when you don't have a boyfriend. During your teenage years, you should enjoy going out in groups with a lot of friends. Most girls have guy friends along with girl friends. Plan a night bowling, or go to the movies. Our Creator has given you the capacity to be creative. So put together a fun evening and invite your friends.

Here are some fun creative ideas girls have shared with me:

- Have everyone in your youth group over to your place to bake cookies for your youth minister and his family. Then deliver them late that same night. Your youth minister will love it!
- Have some friends meet downtown. There are so many fun things to do there. Take a camera along to shoot some crazy pictures with statues and historical locations. You may even take some pictures with people you don't know. Plan to eat somewhere while you're there. On the way home, drop your film off at a one-hour developing center, and be sure to get extra

Be a leader and everyone will love you for it.

pictures developed to share. Then have all the girls stay over, and make a scrapbook from this memorable occasion.

- Play softball.
- Get involved with your neighbors. Do yard work for an elderly woman or new mom in your neighborhood.
- Plan a car wash.
- Play volleyball.
- Have a movie night. Have popcorn and watch a movie that everyone knows the lines to. Disney movies are the best!
- Play cards or Pictionary.

Okay, don't just think about how fun this would be, make a plan! Enjoy! Add your own ideas to the list.

- _____

  _____

- _____

  _____

- _____

  _____

- _____

  _____

- _____

  _____

- _____

  _____

Never Been Kissed

Recently I had the opportunity to hang out with some awesome college girls. We began to talk about things they struggle with at school, and one of the girls asked me if I really thought there are godly guys out there waiting for Miss Right. I told them that I have a great story that answers that question.

A few years ago, I was speaking at a Fellowship of Christian Athletes meeting at a local high school. The topic was "Abstinence Till Marriage." When I finished speaking, a nice-looking young man raised his hand and said, "Ma'am, can I say something to the group?" "Of course," I replied.

"Well ma'am, I am a senior, and I haven't dated since my freshman year. Most of these guys have teased me about it, but I think since graduation is in a few weeks, I should share with them why. Since I can remember, I always had a girlfriend. My freshman year I was dating a girl and realized my thoughts and my actions weren't pure. I prayed about it and made the decision to break up with her and not date again until I felt I was ready. I then made a point to make some changes. I became a leader in my youth group and stayed busy with football practice, homework, and a job. I didn't have much time to think about girls. Oh yeah, I heard about it in the locker room and these friends of mine didn't seem to get it, but I knew girls and dating were something God had told me to walk away from for now.

"It's my senior year, and prom was coming up. I began to pray and asked God if I should take a date. This is the idea He gave me. Three weeks before prom, I

Are there

godly guys

out there?

invited this great Christian girl that I respect very much to be my date. On the way to pick her up I stopped by the store and bought a single white rose. I placed it on the passenger seat of my car where she would soon be sitting. On the way to her house, I prayed that God would keep my thoughts and our conversation pure. I arrived at her house and was greeted by her dad at the front door. We talked a little, then her mom took tons of pictures of us.

"When it was time to go, we walked to my car where I opened the door for her. She saw the rose and smiled. I picked up the rose and held one of her hands and looked at her eye-to-eye. I told her that this white rose stood for purity and as pure as she was when she got in my car would be as pure as she would be when I brought her home. I then told her that I hoped that if someone was taking out my future wife, that I prayed she was getting the same respect from her date. And on my wedding night I plan to fill the honeymoon room up with white roses to show my bride that I kept myself pure just for her."

He said they had a great night and that God had honored his request. He told the group how good it is to have no regrets. He wasn't bragging about this at all. You could see the sincerity on his face and the respect he was getting on the faces of those who heard his story. Wow! What an incredible story. I know you are probably saying, "What an incredible guy! Where can I find him?"

After I shared this story with the college girls, one of them came to me and asked if I could talk with her

Where can I find him?

privately before our night was over. She shared with me how she was always embarrassed about the fact that she was a sophomore in college and had never been kissed. She said that she was starting to wonder what was wrong with her until she heard this story. Now she has a new outlook on life. She now feels blessed that God has kept her in safekeeping when it comes to sexual purity. She realized as the story was being told that God has a great plan for her life and never being kissed was a good thing. Just think what she has saved for her Mr. Right!

I'm sure there are many girls who feel the very same way. I have spoken with thirty-year-old ladies who are starting to wonder if Mr. Right will ever come along.

I have to say that I can't relate to their situation. I had plenty of kisses by the time I was a sophomore in high school. Believe me, I'm not boasting. I'm embarrassed! What a wonderful thing to be able to say you had only kissed your husband. Wow! What an example.

He Likes Me!

Sheryl was a girl who had never had a boyfriend until one day when Lance started showing up at her house. She was flattered that he was coming over, but her parents didn't have a good feeling about it. She was telling me about the young man, and I asked, "So how long have you guys been going out?" She got a funny look on her face and said, "Well . . . we're really not going out, I guess."

"Oh, I see. So y'all are just good friends?"

"Well, I think we're more than friends," she replied.

When he's less than ideal, how do you deal?

"So, is he a Christian? Where does he go to church?" I asked.

Sheryl didn't know the answers to my questions but she looked like she was about to cry.

"Well, you guys haven't kissed or anything, right?" I persisted.

"Yes, we have, and we have even done a little more than that!" she answered defensively. "And he *does* like me, or why would he keep coming over to my house?" she asked sarcastically.

"I'm not sure why, but Sheryl, do you really like this guy or do you just like the fact that he is showing an interest in you?" I questioned.

"Yes, I like him." She quickly responded.

"Sheryl, I think you should **rate your date**," I told her. "You should get a sheet of paper and number two columns, one through ten. On one column list the things you like about Lance, and on the other column write the things you don't. This may help you get a more realistic picture of your new friend."

When Sheryl left, I think she was probably wishing she had never told me about the new guy in her life, but a couple days later when I saw her again, she told me that she was so glad I told her to "rate your date." She said that she could only think of two things she liked about Lance, yet she had 14 answers on the "don't like' side. She went on to tell me that Lance had not been back to her house because she was continuing to blow him off every chance she got.

Rate your date...

Rate Your Date

Things I like about him:

1. _____

2. _____

3. _____

4. _____

5. _____

6. _____

7. _____

8. _____

9. _____

10. _____

Rate Your Date

Things I don't like about him:

1. _____
   _____

2. _____
   _____

3. _____
   _____

4. _____
   _____

5. _____
   _____

6. _____
   _____

7. _____
   _____

8. _____
   _____

9. _____
   _____

10. _____
    _____

GAB Session
~ with Chandra ~

Lord, may the beauty of Your Spirit in me be so evident to others that I would give up everything just to have You. When I sing the psalm, "Better is one day in Your courts than thousands elsewhere," may it be true. Oh God, all I want is You from early in the morning until late at night. Find in me a heart that longs for You. Lord, bless me and let me be patient with Your plans for my life. I love You, Lord, and I know that through faith all things are possible and You want the best for me. Show me today anything I need to give up or release to You so that You will have my whole heart. Lord, show me anything that is taking Your place in my life. I open my heart to You and I ask these things in Jesus' name. Amen

I recently had lunch with a college student I have known for years. She has grown up to become a beautiful and godly young woman. Being on her own, making grown-up decisions every day, she has really experienced a lot in the past three years.

Although a Christian and in church all her life, she wonders why it took her so long to see that having a boyfriend is not the most important thing in life. During a long-time relationship, she felt the Lord saying, "I want to be your first love, your one and only." This young lady asked herself if Jesus was her first love, her one and only, and realized that she had never put Him up front. After much prayer and talking with other Christian sisters she respected and trusted, she broke up with her boyfriend after a very long time together. She said, "The breakup was so hard. I didn't want to hurt this guy. I love him. But this is just an area of my life where I had to honor God." As hard as it was, God has given her complete peace about the decision, and she is confident that in time God will lead her back to this man if he is indeed the one for her.

This is a perfect example of what happens when we have a pure heart. We only want what God wants. Our only desire is to please and obey God no matter what we have to give up.

I can't wait to see what God does in her life. Whether they get back together or marry different people, I am confident that God will bless them more than they can imagine for their pure hearts.

Chandra

My Journal

My Journal

My Journal

session 4

Preparing for Dating God's Way

"But seek first his kingdom and his righteousness,
and all these things will be given to you as well."
–Matthew 6:33

Choosing to stay pure like the untouched snow on a mountain peak is a great choice when thinking about **sexual purity**. Your goals and morals should be so high that no one can touch them. Think "mountain" when you are having trouble getting yourself out of a passionate, heated moment. Don't let the heat of the moment melt the snow.

When I speak to students on dating and sexual purity, I can always count on having everyone's full attention. It seems most students want to know more, but they don't want to be the one to bring it up. Maybe you would like the truth when it comes to dating and relationships with guys. Maybe you have never kissed a boy, but you still want to know what it's like. In this session, I want to help you understand more clearly what the dating life is all about. I'd like to start by helping you develop a *dating tool chest*.

Tool Chest?

Your tool chest is an imaginary box that holds tools of truths from God's Word concerning sexual purity. Stories I'll share, visual ideas I will give, and facts you need to know will prayerfully keep you sexually pure until you marry your Prince Charming—the one God has chosen just for you.

These tools will never rust or give out, but it's up to you to use them. Be sure not to lose or misplace these tools. Now that you are getting older and more mature, you must keep this tool chest with you at all times. The crucial tools you need to have in your tool chest are:

- A knowledge of God's design for true love
- A willingness to listen to the Holy Spirit's guidance in your life
- An understanding of key differences in how guys and girls relate
- Goals that will lead you to God's best for your future

Love! True Love!

Who's interested in that? I bet you are. Girls simply want to know the facts about being "in love." So, let's talk!

There are so many misconceptions about what is right and what is wrong when it comes to sexual issues. I can remember when I was in fourth grade that a fifth grade girl told me that if you French kiss you can get pregnant. Well, thankfully I have learned a lot more about the birds and the bees since the fourth grade. I may be older than you and might not be as hip, but I can tell you one thing for sure—I know about *true love*. I am also sure that God's Word never changes and the dating tips you get in this book will be the truth.

You see students, *true love* is so much more than all this sex that TV, movies, friends, magazines, and music talk about. There really is such a thing as *true love*.

I married my high school sweetheart at age 18, and we have celebrated over twenty years together! I love Bruce very much, and there is no question in my mind that he loves me. The key has been that Bruce and I both put God first in our lives. Our marriage is centered on God's love and His truths. Through that love God enables us to love each other, forgive each other, put the other first and not be selfish, to be giving and sensitive of each other's feelings, to be caring, not jealous or rude, to trust one another and never doubt our commitment to each other, our marriage and our children. God tells us when we put Him first in our lives, He will be the power and strength behind everything else.

The world paints a picture of sex being just another thing to do when you are bored. It is talked about, laughed about, joked about, and cheapened by so many, but I am here to tell you the truth! God made sex good, but He designed sex to be enjoyed within the boundary of marriage.

I have a precious friend who has cancer. She, too, has a love and a passion to teach young girls how important Jesus is in their lives. She also has the desire to teach girls what true love is. While visiting in her home I asked her to share with me so I could share her story with you. This is her story.

What's right and what's wrong?

Marriage is much more than sex.

I have been blessed with true love. My husband loves me and is in love with me. Several years ago, in order for me to live, I had to have one of my breasts removed. Years later, I still have a huge ugly scar and a hole in my side. It is deformed-looking, not attractive at all. Also, as you know, with chemo I am often bald. Doesn't that sound beautiful? Ha! But because my husband loves me so much, he holds me close, kisses me, and tells me I am beautiful. This is a picture of God's unconditional love. Many young girls think love is all about how a person looks on the outside. They dream about handsome guys with muscular bodies. Their perfect guy has a certain color eyes, certain hair, and a particular body type—tall, big shoulders, good hair, etc. I want them to hear my story because they don't understand how important these wedding vows are: "For better, for worse, in sickness and in health, till death do you part." Being faithful and committed to your spouse in these conditions is when you know you have true love. If they would stop and think for a moment about this guy who's a hunk and try to see him bald, a little overweight, sick, with the loss of a body part—would they still love this person? Sex in marriage is good, but marriage is so much more than that. The Bible gives this instruction: "Husbands, love your wives, just as Christ loved the church and gave himself up for her" (Ephesians 5:25). Unconditionally. I have found that in my husband—I have been blessed with true love. I pray that many young girls will be blessed with this kind of love. It can only come from knowing Jesus.

(In memory of my dear friend Shari.)

The love we need to give to our spouse can only come from the love of God. Although couples love each other, marriage is a huge commitment, because there will be times we disagree and have trouble honoring or even loving our mate. It can only work through Jesus.

Marriage vows are designed to never be broken. The Lord God knows that when two people are joined together with Him, there should never be a separation. But 43% of all marriages end in divorce—that's like one in every two—and 60% of all remarriages end in divorce. (Statistics from the Marriage Act, 2003.)

I hope that you can see why I am so passionate about teaching these godly principles. Over the years I have heard so many sad stories from teens who are tossed to and fro, from one parent to the next. Many who read this book will understand will understand more than I do the damage that comes from divorce. Please, listen to what our Creator, our Father, the one who designed marriage, has to say.

When you have sex outside of marriage there are awful consequences. Why not choose to say "no" now before you get into a position where you feel the need to be accepted, or don't know how you feel because your heart is racing in the middle of a heated, passionate moment and you think, "Go for it"?

The time is NOW for you to make goals for your dating life.

First you need to understand the meaning of *love*. In America we love everything. I have actually said, "Oh, I just love everything in my life!" We love our car, clothes,

♥

The love we need to give to our spouse can only come from the love of God.

dog, hamburgers, chocolate, parents etc. Maybe not in that exact order but all the same love. The Greek language breaks it down a little more and you need to understand this before we go any further in this study. (The New Testament was written in Greek, and the authors spoke of four different types of love.)

- *Storge*—family love, fatherly love, provider
- *Phileo*—friendship (best friends)
- *Eros*—erotic love, love for things, lust, infatuation
- *Agape*—unconditional, all-encompassing, God's love, love for people

So many times we think we are in love when in reality we are **in like** or **in lust** (eros love). Look at these statements and you'll see the difference.

Love vs. Lust

Love is forever	Lust is for now
Love is tender	Lust is tense
Love is priceless	Lust is cheap
Love is patient	Lust is impatient
Love satisfies	Lust demands
Love is kind	Lust is selfish

These words should help you realize what love **is** and what it **is not**. Many times young ladies get themselves into a relationship and they feel trapped. They can't break up the relationship because they lack self-confidence. Nine times out of ten, it is infatuation that brought together that couple, not love. What is infatuation?

Infatuation

never lasts!

Infatuation seems to happen all at once. Usually you don't even know the person but you have this idea that you just have to go out with him. Infatuation is jealous, in a hurry, and often sex-centered. Infatuation leads you down a path that is far from your goals and will most assuredly leave you with regrets.

When your heart is saying "Don't do it"...LISTEN!

Trust your inner self. The Holy Spirit lives in you if you belong to Jesus. **The Holy Spirit is:**
• your conscience
• your protector
• your counselor
• your guide

Second, it is very important that you understand how different the male gender is from the female. God made men with leadership qualities so they could be the godly leaders in their family. Men have the desire to work and provide for their family. Men are very visual. They are strong and are fine with having one or two close friends. They think differently than we girls do in many situations.

See if you can relate to any of these statements.

• Guys are very visual and can become aroused just by looking at something or someone.
• Women long for a man to listen to her, to bring her flowers, to hold her hand.

♥

Males and females are different!

- Men like physical intimacy where women like receiving emotional intimacy.
- Women want romance, to be touched and caressed.
- Men are satisfied with intercourse in the sexual relationship.
- Little boys like crashing cars and blowing up buildings—being rough.
- Little Girls like playing mommy and feeding baby—nurturing.
- Men don't have a need for many friends.
- Women: the more friends, the better.
- Men go to the bathroom alone.
- Women take their friends with them.
- If a naked lady walked into a room, all the men would look and want more.
- If a naked man walked in the room, women would turn their head from embarrassment, become flushed, and giggle.
- Men can take care of business over the phone and stick to business.
- Women make a lunch date to discuss things, just to get together.

Guys reach their sexual peak when they're 18 years old, while women don't until they are 30. It's all part of God's balance for a healthy, happy sexual marriage. We will discuss this more when we get into the session concerning sexual immorality.

This tip for choosing a possible spouse has been passed down from generations. Now, I'll pass it on to you: if you want to know how a man will treat his wife, observe how he treats his mother. This rings true with my husband. He always treated his mother with respect. He helped her bring in the groceries, took out the garbage, and did other things to help out because he wanted to please her. For more than twenty years, he has treated me with that same respect. Even more so since I am his wife!

Guys Need Significance

Every guy longs to be significant. I'm guessing most guys have probably had a dream like this: His team is down by two points, there are three seconds left on the clock, and he has the ball. The crowd is cheering and chanting his name. He dribbles the ball toward half court, stops, bounces it one time, and shoots. He scores! The crowd goes crazy. His teammates sweep him off his feet and hold him on their shoulders singing, "We Are the Champions."

Girls Need Security

Girls, we like to feel secure! This is why so many young girls give up their high moral standards during the teen years. They feel insecure, and one way they try to fill that need is to be in the arms of a guy. Statistics show that fathers are the main source of security for little girls. In fact, reports show that teenage girls with a loving father in the home have a greater chance of being a virgin when they graduate from high school. Girls who don't have a father who shows affection look elsewhere to fulfill their need for security. Girls like to be held close, to be cuddled, and to be told they have value.

True significance and the source of real security can only be found in a relationship with Jesus Christ. People will fail you—even those you love the most. We must learn to look to the heavenly Father to fill our needs.

Male or female . . . we are each distinct and unique!

Although we girls will never completely understand men, it's good to recognize how different they really are. Especially when it comes to touch, sight, smell, etc.

The media shows a picture of how a girl meets a boy, they have sex, and everything is great. Well, that is because TV isn't real. What they don't show is what happens in between. The REAL story involves the emotional pain that comes along with sexual intimacy outside of God's plan. Sexuality is so much more than physical. Listed below are examples of other ways to express your sexuality.

- **Physical**—give hugs, tickle, play games, etc. . . .
- **Intellectual**—share hopes and dreams, do homework together, etc. . . .
- **Emotional**—laugh together, understand each other, listen to each other, etc. . . .
- **Social**—go to movies, get groups of people together, go bowling, be creative, etc. . . .
- **Spiritual**—go to church together; attend youth group events, retreats, camps; pray together, serve your community, etc. . . .

Setting Goals That Last a Lifetime

If you haven't thought about goals for dating, then this is a perfect time. After reading the previous pages you should already have an idea of what is important to you.

Before you begin, stop and pray. God may bring something new to your mind. Next, start with this question:

What do you want to be doing in 10-20 years from now?

Do you want to be married, have children, career, etc?

My Hopes and Dreams

_____

_____

_____

_____

_____

_____

_____

_____

_____

_____

_____

_____

_____

_____

Now that you have thought about what is important to you, it's time to think about characteristics and qualities you want in your future mate.

Character and Qualities I Hope to Find in My Future Husband

_____

_____

_____

_____

_____

_____

_____

_____

_____

_____

_____

_____

_____

_____

_____

_____

_____

_____

Lord, may this young daughter understand the importance of Your Word and truth as she goes through this season of her life. Guide, direct, and protect her. May she guard her heart with Your Word and Your love. Help her as she makes plans and prepares for these exciting years of her life. Open her eyes and ears so she can test every situation against Your truth. Help her to seek after the things that glorify You. Lord, I pray that she will confess and receive Your forgiveness in areas she may have already fallen short of Your will for her. Let her be reminded today of Your Word: "He who conceals his sins does not prosper, but whoever confesses and renounces them finds mercy" (Proverbs 28:13). Do not cast her away but renew a right spirit within her. Do not cast her away from Your presence, and do not take Your holy spirit from her, but restore her with the joy of Your salvation (Psalm 51:10–12). Amen

GAB Session
~ with Chandra ~

I guess it is time for me to share my story with you. When I was in my early teens, I was head over heels about a guy in my school. He was a preacher's son, and I just knew he was the one for me. After a heart-ripping breakup, I realized this guy was not the guy I thought he was at all. He was not at all what God had planned for Chandra. So for weeks I cried myself to sleep with pictures in my head of him walking down the hall with one of my good friends. Anyway, my mom felt really bad for me and would do anything to make me feel better and quit crying. What she did next changed my life forever.

One day, a guy I barely knew came to my locker and asked if I'd like to go to a movie with him. Having no interest, I quickly replied that, "I can't date!" This was the only time I ever responded so enthusiastically when telling a rule my parents had made for me. You see, since I didn't want to go out with him, the truth seemed very appropriate. Then he asked, "Would you go with me if you could?" I said, "Yes, but I can't"(wrong answer for this guy).

When I got home and walked through the door, I put my books, purse, and dance team bag down, and then I noticed my mom smiling at me. "What?" I said. My smiling mom began to tell me how she had met a very nice young man, and because she knew him and his parents she told him that I could go to the movie with him. She was very happy and ready for me to hug her, when out of my mouth came words of hatefulness. "You did what? Mom! How could you? I don't even know him, and I sure don't like him." Very disappointed, my mom said I would have to tell him myself when he called to give me the details for our date Friday night. (If you watch *Lizzie McGuire*, you can just see a little comic girl throwing a fit about right now.)

The next three hours I did a lot of thinking and talking to my best friend. I decided to go ahead with the date, because if my mom would let me go out once, chances are I could start dating at 15. To make a really long story shorter, the first date was definitely not the last. This guy melted my heart. We continued to date during my sophomore, junior, and senior years, even though he was in college the last two years of my high school days. On May 5 (just before graduation day), he took me out on a very creative date and asked me to marry him. Since it is more than 20 years later, I think you know my answer was "Yes!" and Bruce Peele has been the most wonderful man in my life.

A brief look at what happened while we dated:

- We went to church together every Sunday and to youth group on Wednesday nights.
- I never gave up my friends and he never gave up his.
- His friends became my friends and my friends became his friends.
- He treated me like a lady from day one.
- He won my heart by respecting me and by being a

gentleman.
- While he went to college, I was very active in my youth group and had a lot of guy and girl friends.
- Bruce went to church with his family but had never accepted Jesus has his personal savior, so only months after we started dating he made that commitment to Christ and was baptized in my church.
- We talked about God's Word together.
- We knew each other's family very well.
- We struggled to be pure (we failed many times while we were dating).
- We talked about what God wanted for us spiritually, emotionally, and physically.
- We talked a lot about boundaries.
- We respected each other.
- We trusted each other (although I have to admit there were times of jealousy).
- We got married when I was 18 and he was 20.
- Our wedding day was February 28, 1981.

I am thankful for a dedicated, godly husband, a loving daddy for my girls, and our commitment to God, each other, and all that God has blessed us with. I know it seems everything turned out great for me, and thanks to God it has. But I sure wish someone had told me more about this "dating thing" before I got involved with any guy. There are things in our relationship I regret and looking back I realize I put my self in a lot of bad situations. I can't imagine how I would feel if I hadn't married Bruce but someone else. Seeing so many marriages fail today in my church and in my family, it is my prayer that God will use this book to help you see how setting goals and preparing for dating is very important.

Note: Please understand that I am not saying it is best for you to fall in love and get married at such a young age. This is just my story.

Chandra

My Journal

My Journal

My Journal

The Dating Game Isn't a Game

"'For I know the plans I have for you,' declares the LORD,
'plans to prosper you and not to harm you,
plans to give you hope and a future.'"
–Jeremiah 29:11

Now that you have set some goals and have a good idea of what you want out of dating and the guy you want to be in that picture, let's talk about some practical things that you need to consider.

The Dating Guide

There is a little man who lives in my computer. He may live in yours too. His name is Dudley Dell, and he is there to help me when I don't know what to do on my computer. I go to him when I need help. How is it that he is able to answer my questions and solve my problems? He designed my computer. He knows it inside and out.

God is the creator of you and me and the sexual feelings we have, so who's better to go to concerning our questions about dating than Him? God's design for fulfilling our need for love and security, as well as for the one we date is perfect. As we begin to date and prepare to meet our lifetime mate, we simply must go to God's Word as our guide.

Putting God first means that we daily love Him with our whole heart, mind, soul, and strength (Luke 10:27).

- How can putting God first affect your dating relationships?
- Why is it so difficult to give Him full control of every detail in our lives?
- Now ask yourself this hard question . . . who is really first in your life?

When praying for His wisdom and direction, consider these:

Who, What, When, Where, Why, and How?

When considering these questions, one has a lot to ponder. As you continue to grow and mature, social dating probably will come into the picture. You may go out on "a" date or go out with the same person on "many dates." Although we use the same word for going somewhere with a guy (a date) as for being a couple (dating), you should recognize there is a big difference. When you go out on a date—for example to a movie, a homecoming dance, or a banquet—it is important to consider all these questions. However, if you are "dating" or "going out" with a person many times because you are boyfriend and girlfriend, you should understand and

♥

*"Seek **first** his kingdom and his righteousness, and all these things will be given to you as well."*

—Matthew 6:33

take seriously your increased responsibility. Whew! That's a mouthful, but I hope that no matter where you live on this planet, you will understand what I am trying to say here.

Dating is when you get to know another person socially, spiritually, and emotionally. Dating does not mean that you become sexually involved with each other. According to God's Word, that is reserved for marriage. When you are on a date, you should guard your heart and your purity.

Some things to think about:
- First, make sure you have goals set.
- Second, what are your expectations for the date?
- Third, know the plan.
- Fourth, don't go on a date "just because." In other words . . . don't settle!

Remember:
- God created marriage to be a special, unique relationship in our lives.
- God has a plan for your life and plans the very best for you. Be patient! Wait for God's best.

"Patience is more than endurance. A saint's life is in the hands of God like a bow and arrow in the hands of an archer. God is aiming at something the saint cannot see, and He stretches and strains, and every now and again the saint says— 'I cannot stand any more.' God does not heed, He goes on stretching till His purpose is in sight, then He lets fly. Trust yourself in God's hands. Maintain your relationship to Jesus Christ by the patience of faith.

♥

Dating does not mean that you become sexually involved with each other.

'Though He slay me, yet will I wait for Him.'" (Job 13:15)

—Oswald Chambers, *My Utmost for His Highest*

Jesus teaches us this same message in the passage of Scripture found in Psalm 46:10—

"Be still, and know that I am God."

and in Isaiah 30:15—

"In repentance and rest is your salvation, in quietness and trust is your strength."

What Is Dating?

The dictionary says a "date" is an appointment to meet someone socially of the opposite sex. You could have one date with a guy or many. In dating there is freedom. You should never allow the relationship to become like a ball and chain.

Chandra's definition: Dating is when two people with interest and attraction for each other get together and have fun! During this time, they find out a lot about each other: their likes, dislikes, family, spirituality, hopes, dreams, and desires. It is purely friendship that *may* or *may not* lead into a time of courtship. It should not become physical unless both people involved discuss their high moral standard. This could lead to holding hands, hugs, and/or kissing, but should never lead to full body contact or touching that causes either to become sexually aroused. Dating should take place in a public or group setting, and be God-honoring at all times.

WARNING!

Dating is designed for getting to know the person better and enjoying each other's company. If you are always crying, always jealous, always upset, have regrets, or are becoming sexually active, then **you need to get out of the relationship.** Realize early in life that you cannot change another person. *God can,* but you can't. Don't stay in any relationship that is bringing you down from your high standards instead of building you up. Life is too short, and you are too young. Remember: Why settle for less?

If your dating relationship becomes more intimate, you may need to reevaluate whether you are still dating or if this relationship become "courting." The only time you court a person is when you are preparing for marriage. Are you ready for that? If not, you should stop, pull back on the reins of the relationship, have a talk with your boyfriend, and determine if you should continue dating.

What Is Courtship Anyway?

Courtship is a time to develop a serious relationship that leads to engagement and marriage. Some people choose to never date. They wait until they are ready to get married and begin a courtship.

Chandra's definition: The relationship has taken a turn. You really are falling in love with this person and want an exclusive relationship with him. You have become emotionally involved in this relationship. Everyone is aware that you are a couple and you should respect each other as such. You need to be assured by

♥

Don't stay in any relationship that is bringing you down from your high standards instead of building you up.

him that he is your guy and show the same kind of respect to him by not flirting with other guys.

The discussion becomes more serious with plans for the future. You are going to church together if you live in the same area, and you pray together often. You take extra precautions to not get into a heated passionate moment because it may get out of control.

Your relationship is still not sexually physical. **Guard your heart.** You two are not "one" until you say "I do." Remind yourself that sex is meant for marriage!

Who Should You Date?

Write a description of a guy you would want to date.

_____

_____

_____

_____

_____

_____

_____

_____

_____

_____

_____

_____

_____

Be Wise!

"Blessed is the man who finds wisdom, the man who gains understanding, for she is more profitable than silver and yields better returns than gold."
—Proverbs 3:13,14

You may have thought about what you want your date to be like; however, if you have left out the following very important truth, you need to go back and rethink your thoughts:

"Do not be yoked together with unbelievers. For what do righteousness and wickedness have in common? Or what fellowship can light have with darkness?"
—2 Corinthians 6:14

Knowing that the young man you choose to date is a Christian should be at the top of your list.

Why is this such an important condition?

_____

_____

_____

_____

_____

_____

_____

What if you're young and just dating? Is it still important? Why?

_____

_____

_____

_____

_____

_____

It is not enough to know that he goes to church or attends youth camp in the summer or that he is a really nice guy. Read Ephesians 5: 6–7:

"Let no one deceive you with empty words, for because of such things God's wrath comes on those who are disobedient. Therefore do not be partners with them."

Give some examples of "empty words."

_____

_____

_____

_____

_____

What are some ways you can bring this up with your friend before you go out with him? You need to be comfortable with these questions and confident when you ask them. I think you

will have a good idea about his spiritual commitment not only by his response but his reaction.

_____

_____

_____

_____

_____

Now that you know why you want to date and _who_ you would like to go out with, let's talk about you for a minute. Answer these three questions—and remember, set your goals high.

What should you wear on a date?

_____

_____

_____

_____

_____

Is what you're wearing a reflection of who you are?

_____

_____

_____

_____

_____

How should you expect to be treated by your date?

_____

_____

_____

_____

_____

Group Dating

Let's be real! When you are dating someone and are very attracted to him, you get those lovey-dovey feelings and imagine yourself in his arms. *That's exactly the point I'm making here!* If that is all that would happen, there would be no problem. But every little moment like that can lead to more. It will, believe me. Most girls are fine with a passionate kiss from their boyfriend, but we have to wake up and smell the coffee here. Those boys are imagining far more than kissing. It's how they are wired. So we have to help them out by understanding how they work.

Chances are good that when you are surrounded with other people on a date, you will have more fun! When I talk to teenagers who have become sexually active, the number one reason they have sex is because they are . . . are you ready for this? Because they are **BORED!** So protect yourself from being bored. When you have other friends around, you're laughing, talking, and involved in whatever the group is doing.

Another really great reason to date in a group is what you can find out about the person you're with.

• How does he act in a crowd?

• How is his language?

- How does he treat you?
- What do others think about him?
- Is he a gentleman?
- Is he Christ-like?
- What is his character?
- Integrity?
- Is he controlling?
- Does he look at other girls when you're with him?

There are many things you can find out about a person when you're in a group. The next time you are out with a group of friends, take notice.

Trust!

In any relationship there must be trust! When you are dating someone, if you can't trust him or he doesn't trust you, look out for problems ahead. Without trust, jealousy comes into the picture and you or he will become consumed with questions and anxiety. Remember, dating is supposed to be fun! If you are dating someone and you begin to see this pattern, you should jump ship now! More importantly, if you are in a serious relationship and this lack of trust persists, look at what God's Word says about love.

"Love is patient, love is kind. It does not envy, it does not boast, it is not proud. It is not rude, it is not self-seeking, it is not easily angered, it keeps no record of wrongs. Love does not delight in evil but rejoices with the truth. It always protects, always trusts, always hopes, always perseveres."
—1 Corinthians 13:4–7

After reading this Scripture, you should really stop and

First things first—

trust the Lord!

think about your relationship. Are you putting this guy before God? God loves you and wants the best for you. Are you settling for less?

Communication

Being able to talk and communicate well to someone you are dating is another very important piece of the puzzle for healthy happy relationships.

- Is he a good listener?
- Does he join in the conversation when you are talking?
- Does he show interest in what you have to share?
- Does he share his feelings with you?

Do you sit around with nothing to say to each other? Look for ways to start up a conversation. Talk about his/your likes, dislikes, how things are at home, etc. . . . If communication continues to be a problem, you may need to rethink this dating relationship. What are you in it for? It doesn't sound like much fun to me.

Praying for Relationships

"And I will do whatever you ask in my name, that the Son may bring glory to the Father. You may ask me for anything in my name, and I will do it."
—John 14:13–14

What is the most significant part of this passage?

_____

_____

_____

_____

❤

"Do not be anxious about anything, but in everything, by prayer and petition, with thanksgiving, present your requests to God."
—Philippians 4:6

This is a good reminder that it's not all about you. It's all about Him (God).

What do you think about your life really being all about Him?

_____

_____

_____

_____

_____

If you are praying for God to bless you with good friendships, start looking around. I believe that when we open our spiritual eyes to see what God's will is for our lives, we will be surprised to see what is directly in front of us.

What opportunities to share Christ are you missing?

_____

_____

_____

_____

_____

I don't think praying for a boyfriend or someone to date is how you should pray. Instead, pray for godly friendships to develop in your life. You never know where these friendships can lead. Be patient! God has promised that He has a plan for your life. Wait on God to write your love story.

Check your motives. Why are you so anxious about having a boyfriend? If you are looking for security in a boyfriend, someone to make you feel better about yourself, you may need to re-examine who you are in Christ. All girls need to feel secure, but we can only find true security in Jesus. Let Jesus be your first love. An intimate relationship with Him will satisfy all your needs.

Many girls will experience going through football season with no homecoming date or no invitation to a special banquet. It seems really bad at the time, but it's not the end of the world. You will have many more opportunities to go to events such as these during your high school and college years. As hard as these times are, be comforted when you remember *Who* you belong to—Jesus!

Psalm 37:4–7 always lifts me up. I think it fits great with this application to keep you on track. This Scripture is another one of God's promises; may it be an encouragement to you.

"Delight yourself in the LORD and he will give you the desires of your heart. Commit your way to the LORD; trust in him and he will do this: he will make your righteousness shine like the dawn, the justice of your cause like the noon-day sun. Be still before the LORD and wait patiently for him."

Break this Scripture down, and recapture each phrase in your own words. Make it apply to you personally.

"Delight yourself in the Lord…"

_____

_____

_____

"Commit your way to the Lord; trust in him…"

_____

_____

_____

_____

"Your righteousness…"

_____

_____

_____

"The justice of your cause like the noonday sun…"
What exactly do you think that means?

_____

_____

_____

"Be still…"

_____

_____

_____

How can this Scripture help you in your dating life?

_____

_____

_____

_____

_____

_____

When Should I Date?

When your parents say you can. There is really no magic
age or time one should start to date. It has more to do
with how mature you are and how responsible you are.
The sad thing is that so many girls start to date before
they have ever considered the truths of God's Word or
the topics of this book. There is a lot to consider when
determining when dating is right for you.

Why do you want to date?

_____

_____

_____

_____

_____

_____

When do you think is a good time and for what reasons?

_____

_____

_____

_____

_____

Where Should We Go?

When planning a night out, whether with a group or as a couple, keep this in mind:

"And whatever you do, whether in word or deed, do it all in the name of the Lord Jesus, giving thanks to God the Father through him."
—Colossians 3:17

Also remember another promise from God. In Exodus 33:14, God promises you will never be alone.

"The LORD replied, 'My Presence will go with you, and I will give you rest.'"

What seems good to you about this Scripture?

_____

_____

_____

_____

What seems not so good about it when you realize that God sees and knows everything? You cannot hide from God.

_____

_____

_____

_____

_____

Check off the places on the list below which would meet the standard given to us in Colossians 3:17.

☐ Youth group events
☐ Parking in a car
☐ Amusement parks
☐ Bowling
☐ Making dinner for your friends or family
☐ Movies with a group of friends
☐ Playing cards
☐ Watching movies late at night
   while your parents are sleeping
☐ Hanging out alone at your house
☐ Skating
☐ Sporting events
☐ Putt-putt golf
☐ A party at a friend's house with no parents present
☐ Camping together with other couples
☐ Stargazing
☐ Community service projects
☐ Baking cookies
☐ Bike riding

Why are some of these ideas clearly inappropriate?

_____

_____

_____

_____

_____

Which ideas are questionable and why?

_____

_____

_____

_____

_____

Father, thank You for designing marriage. Thank You for instructing me on what to do and what not to do for my own sake. Thank You, Father, that even though I don't understand the mystery of two becoming one flesh, I can trust Your words. Someday when I am married to that special man You have prepared for me, I am confident I will understand then, and I can again say thank You. God, it is really weird for me to think about marriage when I know I'm not ready, but help me to see the importance of planning now for that very important day when I will say "I do" to that very special person. Oh God, help me to wait patiently for him. I know that You have a plan for my life because You have told me so. You are my love. You are my life. Fill me up with Your love so I won't give my heart away to another until that day when together we become one flesh joined by Your perfect love. Amen

GAB Session
~ with Chandra ~

Have you been to any weddings lately? I love weddings! The last wedding I attended, I found myself going through my purse searching for a tissue as I watched the beautiful bride clutch the arm of her father as they walked down the aisle. I don't know if the tears were from the music, the memories of my wedding, thinking back to when the bride was just a pre-teen, or the thought of my own daughters someday walking down the aisle. One thing for sure is they were tears of joy as the Spirit of God filled the church, and friends and family gave their blessings to the happy couple. The two would become one in the eyes of God, and we were all witnessing this very special occasion.

As the wedding continued, I was surprised at how different weddings have become. There were pictures on the screen of the bride and groom as they were growing up, displayed to the words of a perfectly fitting song. They spoke personalized words to each other before the wedding vows were repeated, and at the end of the ceremony the newlyweds walked out to a song from a popular movie. How fun! How special! How unique. Planning. Lots of planning to pull this off.

You know, it's the same way with dating. To pull it off "God's way," much planning is advised. Just as any bride wants no regrets on her wedding day, I know you don't want any regrets during these years you'll be dating. Yes, it takes a lot of planning for that unique and special wedding day. In fact, some take over a year to plan—most, six to eight months. The plans you make now for your dating years are even more important because the emotions you go through, the words you speak and the actions you take will greatly impact your BIG DAY! So as I have said, don't wait until it's too late to plan. Get started now, and begin with prayer.

Chandra

My Journal

Plan your dream date... _____

~~~~~~

~~~~~~

~~~~~~

~~~~~~

~~~~~~

~~~~~~

~~~~~~

~~~~~~

~~~~~~

~~~~~~~~~~~~~~~~~~~~~~~~~~~~~~~~~~~~

~~~~~~~~~~~~~~~~~~~~~~~~~~~~~~~~~~~~

~~~~~~~~~~~~~~~~~~~~~~~~~~~~~~~~~~~~

My Journal

My Journal

My Journal

My Journal

Real Love!
It's Worth the Wait!

"Above all else, guard your heart." –Proverbs 4:23

"And the peace of God . . . will guard your heart."
–Philippians 4:7

"Set your hearts on things above." –Colossians 3:1

"Do not let your hearts be troubled." –John 14:1

"A happy hearts makes the face cheerful." –Proverbs 15:13

God wants you to be happy! He has written beautiful love letters to you in the Bible because He wants you to be filled with joy, to live the abundant life! In His Word, He also reminds us about sin that can destroy our lives. The Scriptures above are just a few examples where He tells us to guard our hearts. The sin that we are going to talk about in this session is the sin of **sexual immorality**. There are many young ladies and men who wish they could go back and start over when it comes to their physical and sexual purity. Their main regret is the effect those actions have had on their hearts.

> *"It is God's will that you should be sanctified: that you should avoid sexual immorality; that each of you should learn to control his own body in a way that is holy and honorable, not in passionate lust like the heathen, who do not know God; and that in this matter no one should wrong his brother or take advantage of him. The Lord will punish men for all such sins, as we have already told you and warned you. For God did not call us to be impure, but to live a holy life. Therefore, he who rejects this instruction does not reject man but God, who gives you his Holy Spirit."*
> —1 Thessalonians 4: 3–8

So . . . see the flashing light, hear the warning, wake up, and listen!

"Flee from sexual immorality. All other sins a man commits are outside his body, but he who sins sexually sins against his own body."
—1 Corinthians 6:18

What is morality?
Virtuous conduct (beginning with your thoughts).

List some things that are moral.

_____

_____

_____

_____

_____

What is sexual immorality?
Immorality is anything that is not moral or pleasing to God. It is unholy, unrighteous, impure, and immoral to have sexual relations outside of marriage.

List some things that are immoral.

_____

_____

_____

_____

_____

According to 1 Thessalonians 4:3–8, sexual immorality is a behavior that is not holy and honorable to God. It is rooted in the passionate lust of people who take advantage of others. Many teens and college students, even adults who have affairs, rationalize their sexual immorality by saying, "We didn't go all the way." According to this Scripture, sexual immorality includes much more that sexual intercourse.

In these Scriptures, God is warning us through the letters of Paul to live holy lives, lives that are pure and pleasing to God. In fact, like we read in 1 Corinthians 6:18, we should *flee* from sexual immorality.

Flee means to run, boogie, do a 180! Get the heck out of there!

Christ lives in us, and we belong to Him, but the temptations will still be there. Too bad that when you commit your life to Christ, part of the package isn't, "You will no longer have sexual temptations." Nope! Unfortunately, that isn't what happens. However, the Holy Spirit is **always** with us and is there to guide us. Many dating Christians become tempted with sexual desires. Some decide it's okay to "make out" and "feel each other up" as long as they don't have sexual intercourse. What a lie we have told ourselves! This is nothing more than rationalizing our choice to sin, making excuses to try to feel better about it.

An article in a popular teen magazine was titled: "How to have sex and still be a virgin."

IT'S A LIE!

The article was describing to its young readers how oral sex, fondling one's genital area, and "outercourse" were ways to become sexually aroused and satisfied, **but** you could still keep your virginity. What a lie! How can you brag about being a virgin when you have experienced most of the intimate relations that were designed for married couples? You can't. If you are, then you are lying to yourself.

This is an area that I really want to talk boldly with you about. As a Christian lady and prayerfully your big sister in Christ, I want you to hear the truth concerning these issues. First of all, when you allow someone to touch you in a private area (any area that a two-piece swimsuit covers), be aware of the damage it can do. I have heard some pretty rude comments from guys at teen gatherings when I was a teenager. The truth is when you allow a guy to touch you in these areas it will leave a sense of guilt and regret behind. Also, your mind is like a recording and it will take a long time for those thoughts to leave you.

I have talked with adult married women who have bumped into their old high school or college boyfriends, and they say these intimate moments come back to them. Although they hadn't thought about that person in years, they had flashbacks when they saw the guys' faces. So think about this before you casually allow someone to touch you.

Remember you are **valuable**. Don't give your treasure of purity away so quickly. Guard your heart, and guard

♥

Remember
you are valuable.

your purity. Now that you have set goals and thought about how far is too far for you, I am sure you will make good choices.

The moment you make a physical connection with your boyfriend, the relationship changes. Another thing that happens when your relationship becomes physical is that the focus is taken off the idea of **getting to know you** and is put on the **physical aspects of the relationship.** Before you know it, you are giving this guy all you are emotionally and physically without any commitment. In other words, you are giving him your heart.

Once you give a little, the next time you will give a little more. You can see where this will lead. It's a trap! Don't get too close, or you may get pulled in. **Long-term** relationships are in real danger of getting to the point of no return once they start down this intimate path. If you are in a relationship and you have been together for more than six months, you should have a serious talk about your commitment to remain pure until marriage. Your boyfriend will either respect you or break up with you. If he was expecting the relationship to become more intimate over time (which may include becoming sexually involved), he may be disappointed and break up. You shouldn't be upset but glad that you found this out before you wasted any more time on the relationship. Many times these long-term relationships become habit more than anything else. After six months in a serious relationship, your boyfriend should already be clear on your hopes, dreams, and spiritual commitments. Remember *Who* you belong to!

♥

You shouldn't give your heart to anyone other than your future husband. Someday when you get married you will become one with your husband. Don't confuse yourself by giving your heart away again and again.

What red flags in a long-term relationship should you notice?
(Example: He becomes controlling. He is always jealous.)

_____

_____

_____

_____

_____

When I was growing up, teens were taught that when you are dating, you should "leave room for Jesus." We joked about it, but it's true! In every dating relationship, there should always be room for Jesus. If three is feeling like a crowd, the guy should leave. Your Father is always with you and He will never leave you.

What are some examples of leaving room for Jesus?
When you kiss?
(Your bodies aren't in a lovemaking position because Jesus is in the middle.)

_____

_____

_____

_____

_____

_____

When you're sitting next to each other?

(You're not like . . . on him.)

_____

_____

_____

_____

_____

_____

What is good about these two statements?

1. Remember Who you belong to!

_____

_____

_____

_____

_____

_____

2. Leave room for Jesus!

_____

_____

_____

_____

_____

_____

If you and all the other people in the world could grasp what God is teaching us through the Scriptures we have studied in this session, we would have much happier lives. God is saying to us, "Okay, I know you are going to sin against Me, but will you really choose to bring consequences to your own body because of sexual sin?" And guess what? We do!

Read 1 Corinthians 6:18 again and consider what is teaching you.

"Flee from sexual immorality. All other sins a man commits are outside his body, but he who sins sexually sins against his own body."

When you consider the statistics of failed marriages today, you'll see that 43% of all marriages end in divorce. I think you would agree that this is a direct consequence of sexual immorality in our world today.

What are some other issues we have in our world because of immorality?

_____

_____

_____

_____

_____

_____

_____

There is so much sexual content in the world today. It has always been around, but now it is so easy to get–Internet, television, music, etc. Where do you see or hear about sex most in your world?

_____

_____

_____

_____

_____

Does sexual content in the media affect your decision-making? If so, how? If not, how do you keep from allowing these messages to affect your moral decisions?

_____

_____

_____

_____

_____

What does 1 Corinthians 6:18 mean by sinning against your own body?

_____

_____

_____

_____

_____

What consequences can one have when participating in sex outside of marriage?

_____

_____

_____

_____

_____

Let's talk about those consequences for a minute.
• Out-of-wedlock pregnancy
• Sexually transmitted diseases (STD)
• Cancer
• Genital warts that can be passed on to your children
• Dealing with the question in your mind as you wonder if you are pregnant or if you have contracted an STD

Those are just a few of the **health risks**. But what about the pain sexual immorality brings to your **heart**—the emotional and psychological scars it leaves behind after a moment of heated passion?
• Feeling used
• Reputation being ruined
• Guilt
• Regret
• Low self esteem/ self worth
• Feeling alone and abandoned
• Living with a broken heart
• Living with the pictures in your mind
• Seeing him with someone else

♥

Thank You, Jesus,

for restoring

broken hearts.

This list could go on forever. Just ask someone who has been there. When you choose to be sexually immoral outside of marriage, you are heaping trouble onto your life. Not only am I talking about the physical risk you are taking with your body, but also the psychological effects sexual activity has on your mind.

I have talked to so many girls who have regrets. They wish they could take it all back and have a new start. The scars that sex outside of marriage leaves behind are deep. God will forgive you, but as He warned in 1 Corinthians 6:8, *this is a sin you commit against your own body.* You can never replace what you have given away.

Over time God can heal your wounds, and through your repentant heart, He will restore you and make you whole again. Think about the story of Humpty Dumpty, who sat on the wall. Remember, he had a great fall. All of the king's horses and all of the king's men couldn't put Humpty back together again. You may feel like Humpty after you've given a part of yourself away. You may feel terrible and hurt because you can't find a way to put the pieces back together again. I have good news for you. The **King** can put you back together again. Look to Him for restoration.

Pink and Blue Make...

If you have some pink, blue, and orange construction paper handy, take a minute to go and get it, along with some glue.

This illustration has been the best one I have seen when showing God's plan for sexual intercourse.

Name your blue paper "Jack" and the pink paper

♥

When you are on a date, you may want to have this thought playing through your mind: "I'm not going to do anything with a guy that I wouldn't want my future husband to be doing with another girl."

"Jill." Jack and Jill have a very familiar story. They have been dating for six months and really like each other a lot! They even say, "I love you" before hanging their phones up at night. They have decided since they love each other and have been together for so long, it's okay for them to have sex.

• Now, with the glue, write in big letters "SEX" on the **blue paper**.
• Next, lay the **pink paper** onto the **blue paper** and rub them together to insure a good bonding.
• Leave them alone for about three minutes.
• Come back to them, and tear them apart.
• Notice that there is pink on the blue and blue on the pink.
• Next, put the Jill aside (pink paper) and pick up the **orange paper**, "Sue."
• Now, write the word "SEX" onto the **orange paper** and lay it on the **blue paper**, "Jack."
• Again leave them together for three minutes or so.
• Come back and tear them apart.
• You have just witnessed a very sad thing.

You see, Jack and Jill had sex. Then several days later, for who knows what reason, Jack broke up with Jill, leaving her alone and brokenhearted. It wasn't too long after Jack broke up with Jill that Sue came into his life. Since Jack had already lost his virginity, he didn't see anything wrong with having sex with Sue. Sue had already lost her virginity, so . . . why not?

Your blue paper "Jack" not only has pieces of pink and orange stuck to it, but also part of every other guy

Sue has ever slept with. And Sue not only has a piece of Jack but also Jill. Sue doesn't even know Jill. And now, none of these pieces of paper will ever be whole again.

One or more of the papers may also have holes in them. This is a perfect picture of what happens when sexual intercourse takes place. To go a little farther, I believe that any sex act leaves behind pieces of those involved.

A few weeks later Sue breaks it off with Jack, and he starts to feel bad about what he has done. He doesn't want to carry this baggage around every moment, so he prays to God and repents. He wants to start over and prays for God to forgive him.

Now place a white paper over the blue paper.

This is a beautiful picture of what God does for you and me through Jesus—not by our works, but by His grace. The blood He shed on the cross paid the debt for all your sin—past, present, and future. Thank You, Jesus, for restoring broken hearts.

Back to the story . . .

That night, Jack calls Jill and asks her to forgive him. He explains to her what Jesus has done in his life, and they talk. Jill is able to sleep that night after she, too, asks the Lord to forgive her and make her whole and clean again.

Maybe you can share this illustration with a friend, or perhaps you needed healing and restoration.

Take a few minutes to pray and ask God to forgive you of your sin. Ask God to show you if you are having immoral thoughts or involved in other moral issues that

Any sex act leaves behind pieces of those involved.

could lead to severe consequences in your life? Share your heart with Him.

Our God is a God of second chances. Only by His grace!

The Car of Your Dreams

You're lying on the couch after school, watching your favorite show, "Oprah," enjoying your time of no interruptions, when you hear the door open. It's your dad.

"Hey Dad, what are you doing home so early?"

"Well, Sugarpie, I wanted to surprise you. Grab your shoes and meet me outside; we're going to get your birthday present—a new car!"

You can't believe what he just said, and the look on your face shows it.

"Really, let's go, honey," Dad says

Well! This is no time for Oprah! You're going to get a new car! You amazingly beat your dad to the car. You drive down to the car dealership that has "the car of your dreams," and the color you want is sitting right out front. Your dad parks, and you get out and walk—trying not to run—over to the car. You turn around to say something to your dad, but he's not there. You notice he has walked over to the other side of the car lot.

"Hey Dad, over here!"

He waves his hand for you to come where he is. Your heart is starting to sink a bit because he's looking at this used car that you certainly didn't have in mind.

"Honey, what do you think about this one? It was in the paper, and the price is right. Let's take it around the block."

"Okay, Dad," you reply solemnly.

"These cars take a lot of wear and tear, and I hear they can get up to 200,000 miles before they quit running. This one only has 105,000," he observes as you drive the car. You're noticing the paint job and the green color, and you can't help but notice the smoky, mildew smell. You're trying not to complain, but your stomach is grumbling with disappointment.

"Yeah, Dad, it's okay."

"What's wrong honey, you don't like it?" asks your dad, who notices your disappointment. "Was there another car you had in mind?"

"Well, I know it probably costs too much, but when you said 'new car'—it's the one I've always dreamed of."

Your dad pulls back into the car lot, and you point out the shiny red sports coupe.

"Well, let's go over and look at it and take it for a drive," Dad says with a smile on his face.

After the drive, your dad hands you the keys and says this to you: "Sweetie, you're my girl, my daughter, and I love you so much. Since you were born you have given me such joy. You have been obedient to your mom and me and have shown us the respect every parent hopes for. It pleases me to provide for you and make you happy. Happy Birthday, Sweetie!"

Wow! What a story. I know that every dad can't be this extravagant, but godly daddies desire to provide for their children and make them happy. How much more does God want to do for you? I think it is inconceivable.

"It is God's will that you should be sanctified [holy]: that you should avoid sexual immorality."
—1 Thessalonians 4:3

The car of your dreams is brand new. It doesn't have scratches and dents. The new seats have never been sat in, so you get to make your personal indentations in them. You won't let people use your car because it is yours, and you want to take good care of it. You are responsible for what happens to it.

Now let me apply this story to your sexuality and your future. If you are sexually pure, you are brand new, never been touched. You don't have the scars that sex outside of marriage leaves behind. You don't have to worry about what others have left behind, because you have guarded your heart and will leave only your impression when you give yourself to your husband on your wedding night. You have the responsibility to yourself and your future mate to protect your purity. Because of this commitment, you won't allow your body to be used.

What Guys Think

When I am speaking to coed groups about abstinence and I ask this question to the guys—"What is the wife of your dreams like?"—the response I get is: "caring, trustworthy, clean, neat, ladylike, godly, prays for me, respects me, needs me, happy, not critical, works with me, makes me look good, committed to me, a godly mom, a good cook, fun, good sense of humor, etc."

"How many of you want the 'bright shiny new one' when it comes time to choose a wife?" The girls in the crowd see for themselves. These guys desire a virgin—the bright shiny new one, the one who has never belonged to anyone else.

Of course, some of these guys may have lost their

virginity or have at least been sexually active to some degree. So their response is great to see when I ask the girls the same question. My question to you now is the same:

What is the husband of your dreams like?

_____

_____

_____

_____

_____

_____

Do you want the bright shiny new one? The virgin?
Why have you given this answer?

_____

_____

_____

_____

_____

What a great eye-opener for both males and females—to see that **98%** of us want what is pure. There are no substitutes for purity. Anyone can give away their virginity, but no one can get it back.

♥

There are

no substitutes

for purity.

_____

_____

_____

_____

_____

"The Lord God said, 'It is not good for the man to be alone. I will make a helper suitable for him.' Now the Lord God had formed out of the ground all the beasts of the field and all the birds of the air. He brought them to the man to see what he would name them; and whatever the man called each living creature, that was its name. So the man gave names to all the livestock, the birds of the air and all the beasts of the field.

But for Adam no suitable helper was found.

So the Lord God caused the man to fall into a deep sleep;

One with Christ

The Holy Spirit lives in those who accept Christ Jesus. We become one with Him. We are the temple of God because that is where He lives.

Let's look at 1 Corinthians 6:15–17:

"Do you not know that your bodies are members of Christ himself? Shall I then take the members of Christ and unite them with a prostitute? Never! Do you not know that he who unites himself with a prostitute is one with her in body? For it is said, 'The two will become one flesh.' But he who unites himself with the Lord is one with him in spirit."

You saw clearly in the construction paper illustration how two become one. We become one with the person to whom we give ourselves sexually. That was the whole point when God came up with sexual intercourse—**that two should become one**. We were not made to become joined together (which the act of sexual intercourse does) and then be pulled apart from one another. The bonding that is created between two people during the act of sexual intercourse does just that: it bonds us together.

When you glue something together, the intent is to never take it back apart, right? So why, knowing this truth, do so many give in to sexual temptation?

Stop and pray!

- That God would renew your mind
- That He would help you turn from the "popular" ways of others
- That He would transform your mind so that you could know His good and perfect will for your life

How can you know God's will for your life?

_____

_____

_____

_____

_____

Write about a time when you knew God's will for a particular situation.

_____

_____

_____

_____

_____

and while he was sleeping, he took one of the man's ribs and closed up the place with flesh. Then the Lord God made a woman from the rib he had taken out of the man, and he brought her to the man.

The man said,
'This is now bone of my bones
and flesh of my flesh;
she shall be called
"woman,"
for she was taken out of man.'

For this reason a man will leave his father and mother and be united to his wife, and they will become one flesh. The man and his wife were both naked, and they felt no shame."
—Genesis 2:18–25

In times of searching for God's will, what do you do?

_____

_____

_____

_____

_____

♥

God wants

the best for us.

"So God created man in his own image, in the image of God he created him; male and female he created them. God blessed them and said to them, 'Be fruitful and increase in number; fill the earth and subdue it. Rule over the fish of the sea and over every living creature that moves on the ground.'"
—Genesis 1:27–28

As Christians we are called to a higher standard of living. Yes, we will be tempted. Our bodies are made with the desire to want love. However, in Genesis 1:27–28 and Genesis 2:18-25 (in the margin), it is clear that the purpose of sexual intimacy was designed for husband and wife. It is also God's purpose for husband and wife to replenish the earth. God wants the best for us, and he knows it is best for us to yield to His design for sexual intimacy.

After understanding what the Bible teaches about morality, you should pray and seek His Word for direction. Set boundaries early so you'll be ready to use them if and when necessary.

"Blessed is the man who perseveres under trial, because when he has stood the test, he will receive the crown of life that God has promised to those who love him."
—James 1:12

Sex is worth the wait, and you are worth waiting for!

God's design for sex is a beautiful expression of love between a husband and a wife. When we engage in sex outside God's plan, we tarnish the image and character of God for our partner and ourselves.

Abstinence Till Marriage

Save Sex, It's Worth the Wait!

Did You Know . . . ?

- Anyone can have sex. Even dogs have sex. How many differences can you think of between humans and dogs? There are many. Dogs act on instinct. Humans have self-control. You can be strong and overcome your temptation because of Christ, who lives in you. A person with self-control, self-respect, and self-discipline can overcome sexual desires.

- When you choose to be sexually abstinent until marriage, you are free to go for your hopes and dreams.

- Teenage girls are more susceptible to STD's than anyone else because their immune systems and reproductive systems are not fully developed.

- The Human Papilloma Virus (HPV) is the most common of all STDs in the U.S. This virus also can cause cancer, killing about 5,000 women each year. This virus is incurable and can be asymptomatic or come in the form of genital warts. This virus is spread though the sexual area of the body and can be contracted through skin-to-skin contact.

• Genital herpes is an incurable virus that causes painful blisters and sores around the sexual area. These sores can come back over and over, again and again throughout your lifetime. It is very contagious and can be passed on when no visible symptoms can be seen! It can be fatal to newborn babies.

• Chlamydia is the number one bacterial STD in America. Since most infected girls are asymptomatic, this disease is known as the silent sterilizer. This STD is curable, but the damage can last a lifetime.

• Sex is the most intimate form of bonding known to mankind.

• When drugs and/or alcohol are in the picture, students are more likely to give in to sexual desires.

• Most teenagers have not had sex!

• "When you have sex with someone, you are having sex with everyone they have had sex with for the last ten years, and everyone they and their partners have had sex with for the past ten years."
—C. Everett Koop, former U.S. Surgeon General

GAB Session
~ with Chandra ~

Have you ever accidentally broken a glass at dinner? Embarrassing, right? At my house, if someone breaks a glass, I quickly sweep it up and throw it into the trash. (It can easily be replaced.) My biggest concern is for the person, so while sweeping I say to them, "It's okay. It's just a glass. Don't worry about it." However, one time, a very special antique plate was knocked off the wall by a guest, and I tried so hard not to let them see the disappointment on my face. I fell to my knees, desperately trying to find every tiny little piece with hopes of restoring it back to its original beauty.

Isn't it great to know that Jesus is in the restoration business? When I consider that He gave His only Son so we could be assured forgiveness, I think restoration is one of His favorite things to do for His children.

"And the God of all grace, who called you to his eternal glory in Christ, after you have suffered a little while, will himself restore you and make you strong, firm and steadfast. To him be the power for ever and ever. Amen."
—1 Peter 5: 10–11

When we suffer from regret, guilt, or remorse, it sometimes seems like we will never be free from pain. Isn't it wonderful to know that God willingly and freely, without question, is waiting for us to call on Him for restoration?

Thinking back on that plate I put back together, up close anyone could see that it had been glued, and there were a few missing pieces. But when God, the Creator, restores one of His children, His restoration is flawless. No glue marks can be seen. The touch of the Master's hand is unexplainable. The mystery of His healing and forgiving touch somehow makes us even stronger.

"Great is our LORD and mighty in power; his understanding has no limit."
—Psalm 147:5

If you feel like that used, beat-up old car we talked about earlier, but long to be bright, shiny, and new again, why not ask the Master to touch you and heal you today?

Being restored is being renewed.

Chandra

My Journal

My Journal

My Journal

My Journal

My Journal

Last GAB Session
~~ with Chandra ~~
For Those Who Have
Regrets

"For the grace of God that brings salvation has appeared to all men. It teaches us to say 'No' to ungodliness and worldly passions, and to live self-controlled, upright and godly lives in this present age." –Titus 2:11-12

If you don't decide how far you are going to go on a date, then you may very well end up going too far. There is freedom when boundaries are in place.

Just as a goldfish is very safe and content inside its fishbowl, sex inside the boundaries of marriage is safe. However, if you take the fish out for any extended period of time, it will surely die. Inside the fishbowl there are a lot of freedoms. It might seem boring and that the fish would get tired of doing the same old thing, etc., but it is safe. Outside the bowl might look tempting, fun, and free, but there is danger. The danger includes death.

Inside of marriage there are many freedoms, yet stepping outside of that protective shell leaves you exposed to potential disease, infertility, emotional damage, heartache, and yes, a broken, guilty, scarred heart!

Thinking ahead is a must!

What are some boundaries others have set for you?

_____

_____

_____

_____

_____

_____

_____

Have you already set some personal boundaries in other areas of your life? What about where drugs, alcohol, and smoking are concerned?

_____

_____

_____

_____

_____

_____

_____

Once you have set boundaries for your sexual purity, you still need to guard your heart. In 1 Peter 5:8, the Bible says,

"Be self-controlled and alert. Your enemy the devil prowls around like a roaring lion looking for someone to devour. Resist him, standing firm in the faith, because you know that your brothers throughout the world are undergoing the same kind of sufferings."

The rest of that chapter is awesome. Peter goes on to say,

"And the God of all grace, who called you to his eternal glory in Christ, after you have suffered a little while, will himself restore you and make you strong, firm and steadfast. To him be the power forever and ever. Amen."

What particular areas do you struggle with, and how can having boundaries that you set for yourself guard you from falling into sexual sin?

_____

_____

_____

_____

_____

_____

_____

_____

"For the grace of God that brings salvation has appeared to all men. It teaches us to say 'No' to ungodliness and worldly passions, and to live self-controlled, upright and godly lives in this present age, while we wait for the blessed hope— the glorious appearing of our great God and Savior, Jesus Christ, who gave himself for us to redeem us from all wickedness and to purify for himself a people that are his very own, eager to do what is good."

— Titus 2:11–14

The most commonly asked question from students when I speak on dating is, "How far is too far?" Chances are, if you are asking that question, whatever you are doing or are thinking about doing is too far. If you are pursuing a life of purity, you should not have to ask how far is too far. If you desire a life of purity, you should instead ask, "How far can I run away from sin to get me closer to God?"

The world pulls us one way and God's truth another. When you get closer and closer to sin until you are standing on the line that separates right from wrong, Satan will have little work to do to pull you overboard. Why, as Christians knowing the truth, do we go so far as to dip our big toe into the powerful pulls of temptation? That is why we need a Savior. We simply must seek His direction for our lives daily. When you're facing temptation, read Titus 2:11–14 for encouragement.

The power of Christ lives in you and comes from the Holy Spirit. When Christ died and rose again, He rescued us from all sin. Our hope is in Him. We are no longer a slave to our sinful nature but free and alive because of Christ Jesus.

Who does Titus 2:11 say God's grace has appeared to?

_____

_____

_____

_____

_____

_____

What does His power teach us and give us the strength to do?

_____

_____

_____

_____

_____

Did this happen only in the days when Paul wrote this passage?

_____

_____

_____

_____

_____

What does he say in these verses that applies to our lives today?

_____

_____

_____

_____

_____

What hope does he give you as a Christian?

_____

_____

_____

_____

_____

_____

In Titus 2:14, what does it clearly say Christ did for us?

_____

_____

_____

_____

_____

_____

Who is He purifying us for and what is His desire for us?

_____

_____

_____

_____

_____

_____

When you understand there are consequences when you disobey God's Word in the area of sexual immorality, doesn't it

make it easier to say "No"? What are your thoughts?

_____

_____

_____

_____

Determine now where you will say "Stop!" Add to the list below the benefits of waiting until marriage to have sex.

- Because I'm not ready
- Because God's plan for me is to be married
- Because I don't want to disobey God
- Because I don't want to disobey or hurt my parents
- Because it could destroy my hopes and dreams
- Because I have the right to say "No"
- Because I want to be respected
- Because I want to enjoy being a teenager/college student
- Because I don't want the added emotional stress

- _____
- _____
- _____
- _____
- _____
- _____
- _____
- _____

♥

What are your reasons

for waiting?

This Is Reality

Occasionally, I have the opportunity to speak to teen moms. These girls are between the ages of 14 and 19 and are either pregnant or have babies already. When I leave these girls, my heart aches for them. When I asked them if they would answer some questions that I could share with other girls their age, they were happy to. They hoped their stories would help others. My first question was, "What would you say to a girl who is thinking about having sex with her boyfriend?" The responses were immediate and emphatic: "Wait!" "Don't do it!" "It's not worth it!" "You'll regret it later!"

Jessica was so overcome with the questions she had to leave the room. When she came back, she began to share her story with me.

"There are so many problems and struggles that come after sex that I had never thought about. I am fourteen, but I was thirteen when I had my son. I live with my grandmother in a tiny one-bedroom apartment. I have no privacy."

Tears flowing from her eyes, she continued: "There is always a strain at home because I need help with the baby. I want to finish school, so just getting up in the morning after being up and down with the baby all night is very hard. Then when the baby goes to sleep at night, I get my homework done, so it's late by the time I go to bed.

"Friends? What friends? Once I had the baby, my friends were too busy hanging out and doing regular kid things. They certainly didn't want a crying baby around. I have to always worry about finding a baby sitter if I go anywhere, even to go to school some days if my grandmother has plans. I use to think about saving money to buy a new outfit or just to go to a movie; now I have to think about the baby first and spend what little money I have taking care of him. Formula and diapers are very expensive, so most the time that's all I can afford with the money I get from the government. So was it worth it? No! I lost my virginity to someone who doesn't care about me, much less his son. He is out being a normal teenager, playing sports, having his mom cook and clean for him. He goes out with friends and has no responsibilities. It doesn't seem fair since we both made the choice. I guess I am paying for that choice now, and it looks like I will the rest of my life. I'm going to try my best to finish high school."

She had to stop speaking because she was crying so hard. The room was filled with tears, as they all seemed to be able to relate to Jessica's story. Regret and despair created a very heavy presence in the room that day. This is the reality that movies and television programs never show. I pray that you will take time to consider Jessica's story. Reality TV? *This is the reality* of the consequences of sex outside of marriage!

Living with Regret

Regret is a terrible thing to live with. Think back on things you have regretted in your life, then imagine the regret that Jessica shared. It's sad, but you only understand the heaviness of regret once it's too late.

Are you living with regret that is consuming your life? We tend to push the memories of regret deep in the back of our mind, but somehow these regrets come back to the front of our mind at unexpected times throughout our life. Often, regret doesn't only bring up the pain once or twice, but over and over again.

Just like sin, regret can keep a wedge between you and God. God never leaves you; however, feelings of guilt and regret will keep you from approaching Him with your problems. If you don't deal with regret, it can consume your thoughts and take over your life. Regret can quickly dig its heels into your heart and make a stronghold in your life. Strongholds are a tool of Satan and will rob you of joy and peace.

In Matthew 11:28–30, God's Word gives us hope and comfort once again.

"Come to me, all you who are weary and burdened, and I will give you rest. Take my yoke upon you and learn from me, for I am gentle and humble in heart, and you will find rest for your souls. For my yoke is easy and my burden is light."

Who does Jesus invite to come to Him?

_____

_____

What is the significance of "rest" in this scripture?

_____

_____

_____

_____

_____

What is a yoke? *A yoke is a wooden crossbar that links two load-pulling animals together.* The two mules or oxen work together as they pull the heavy load or a plow. The yoke distributes the weight evenly on both animals.

How does a yoke compare to your regret?

_____

_____

_____

_____

_____

What a picture of God's love! He will not only take your burden and carry it for you—He has already done it.

Has there been a time when you needed God to carry your load for you? You just couldn't go on the way you were. Maybe that time is now.

Is there something heavy in your life today that you need to give to God and allow Him to carry?

_____

_____

_____

_____

_____

In 2 Corinthians 7:10, what kind of heart do godly sorrows bring?

*"Godly sorrow brings **repentance** that **leads** to **salvation** and **leaves no regret**, but worldly sorrow brings death."* (emphasis mine)

Answer the questions the Scripture asked here in 2 Corinthians 7:11.

"See what this godly sorrow has produced in you: what earnestness, what eagerness to clear yourselves, what indignation, what alarm, what longing, what concern, what readiness to see justice done. At every point you have proved yourselves to be innocent in this matter."

What does godly sorrow produce in you?

_____

_____

_____

_____

_____

_____

A heart that repents is one that is ready to admit wrong doing, while worldly sorrow says, "Man, I can't believe I got caught."

I'm afraid we have all been guilty of the worldly sorrow.

Is there a time you can remember having worldly sorrow when you got caught? What was your attitude?

_____

_____

_____

_____

_____

_____

Worldly sorrow pulls you away from God.

Godly sorrow draws you closer to God.

Notice the gift of God's grace in 2 Corinthians 7:10.
It leaves you with no _____.

This, my friend, is the joy of salvation!

Chandra

Dearest Little Sister,

Now that you have finished your journey through this book, ask yourself these questions:

- Is your relationship with Jesus different, and if so how?
- What changes has God asked you to make?
- Do you love and accept who you are as a daughter of the King?
- Have you looked ahead to your future?
- Have you set boundaries and planned ahead for dating?

Now, the most important question I want to ask you is this . . .

Do you know how much God loves you?

Although I may not know you, I have prayed for you many times, and you will continue to be on my heart. My prayer for you is that you have become better acquainted with Jesus and understand that He has a plan for your life. Whether this study was a refresher course or something brand new, it is my prayer that you have a new confidence in who you are because of who He is. The power of God is in you! When you are weak, He is strong. When you feel alone, He is with you. When you feel there is no hope or no way out, your hope is found in Him. Oh little sister, may the Lord bless you and keep you all the days of your life. May you be so close to Him that you hear His Spirit speak to you and guide you.

Three important things I wish I would have understood much earlier in life:

1. **Humility**—Having a humble heart is one others notice and one that glorifies God.
2. **Gentle spirit**—A gentle spirit brings warmth and understanding to others; peace always flows.
3. **Faith**—Faith is living a life believing in God to answer your prayers and provide for your needs, then being confident to live it out. Wow! It's life changing!

May you be blessed with a happy heart, freedom, peace, eternal security, good health, no regrets, the man of your dreams—God style—and always . . . the joy that only Jesus can bring!

Until we meet again,
Love,

Chandra

Questions and Answers

Q—I've been dating this guy for three years, and we will both graduate from college within a year. I'm pretty sure I am getting an engagement ring this Christmas. Since I know we are going to get married, and I know he loves me and I love him, is it okay for us to become sexually active as long as we don't go all the way until we are married?

—Ready for some passion,
College student

A—Dear "Ready for some passion,"

I hate to give you the bad news, but if you are a Christian, then I think you already know what my answer is going to be. I know it is hard, and I can promise you it will only get harder to resist the temptations while engaged. You two really need to pray about and come up with a plan you can live with. I had a friend who thought the same thing. Regretfully, her fiancé was killed the night before their wedding. She regrets that after waiting all that time, they lost their virginity to each other only weeks before the day he was killed. Her advice: **"You don't know he's yours till he says 'I do.'"**

Q—My boyfriend and I are both Christians and leaders in our youth group. We have messed up sexually and have done way more than we should have. Although I really think I love this guy, I have regrets about the things we have done. Can you give me some advice on how to back track?

—Back tracking,
High school student

A—Dear "Back tracking,"

I am so proud of you for taking a step and having the desire and commitment to stop your actions. My advice to you is to tell your boyfriend that you need to make some serious changes in your relationship. Think about the times you make out, and stay away from those opportunities. Many times things happen right in your own house. You know where and when you have the most temptation, so . . . flee from those places. Change your surroundings and never be alone. If you can be committed to what your heart is telling you, I think you can stay with the guy. If not, you may need to break it off for awhile. Test your relationship. Will it still be there without the heated passionate moments?

If you stand on the train tracks when a train is coming, you will be run over unless you GET OFF THE TRACKS!

Q—My boyfriend and I lie on the couch at my house and watch TV almost every Friday night. Do you think this is okay? I think the temptation is growing.

—Help!
College student

A—Dear "Help,"

I think you are onto something concerning the level of temptation in your living room. Why put yourself in that situation when you know that things are getting heated up? What things, exactly? I think you know the answer to that. Remember…

"Men are like microwaves; Women are like crock-pots!"

If you are honest with yourself, you can probably admit that you like the comfort and the security of lying close to your boyfriend. But I'm almost certain his mind is going another direction. Remember, you want to please the Lord. With that in mind, a godly young lady wouldn't want to tease or lead her boyfriend on.

I say change your position and sit up. You can enjoy watching TV sitting side by side.

Q—I want to date and my parents say I'm not mature enough. What can I do to get them to lighten up?

—Desperate,
Freshman/High school student

A—Dear "Desperate,"

This is a really tough question because, honestly, all parents get my support on their decision. As you grow up and mature, you aren't the only one who experiences change. Parents are often afraid of being needed less and seeing you less. My advice to you is first, obey and respect your parents. They are protecting you, and some kids would give anything for that kind of response. Second, talk to them about their concerns and what they think is mature enough. Third, you have plenty of time to date. Go out in groups, have friends over, and enjoy being young. If your actions prove dependable and responsible, you'll probably begin to see them become more relaxed.

My Journal

My Journal

~~~~~~

~~~~~~

~~~~~~

~~~~~~

~~~~~~

~~~~~~

~~~~~~

~~~~~~

~~~~~~

~~~~~~

~~~~~~

~~~~~~

~~~~~~

~~~~~~

My Journal

My Journal

~~~~~~

~~~~~~

~~~~~~

~~~~~~

~~~~~~

~~~~~~

~~~~~~

~~~~~~

~~~~~~

~~~~~~

~~~~~~

~~~~~~

~~~~~~

My Journal